COUNTRY LIFE
Vegetarian Cookbook

Delicious recipes from the kitchens of the Country Life vegetarian restaurants.

Edited by Diana J. Fleming

Contributors include:

Avis Ashton
Arthur Brodie
Sylvia Crary
Roberta Krause

Carol Marno
Jo Ann Rachor
Jennifer Schwirzer
Candace Sweet

Family Health Publications LLC
8777 E. Musgrove Hwy.
Sunfield, MI 48890

The story of this cookbook goes back to 1966 when the first Country Life Restaurant opened its doors in Grand Rapids, Michigan. Today the fifteen Country Life Restaurants, though all independently owned, share a common commitment to serve delicious, wholesome, 100 percent vegetarian food. They are also dedicated to furnishing educational programs, to ministering to the needs of the community and to providing a relaxed, Christian atmosphere as a refuge for customers from the stresses of the work-a-day world. Each restaurant is run by a staff of Seventh-Day Adventists. Country Life staff all over the country and abroad have been experimenting for years to develop and constantly improve delicious and healthful recipes. The fruit of their labors is found within the pages of this book. We heartily recommend it to you.

The Publishers

ISBN 1-878726-00-5

Library of Congress Catalog Card Number 90-81276

First Printing 1990

Printed in the United States of America

Family Health Publications LLC
8777 E. Musgrove Hwy.
Sunfield, MI 48890

TABLE OF CONTENTS

COUNTRY LIFE RESTAURANTS AND STORES

Country Life
200 High Street
Boston, Massachusetts 02110
617 951-2534

Country Life
3748 Ringgold Road
Chattanooga, Tennessee 37412
423 622-2451

County Life
1217 Eberhart Avenue
Columbus, Georgia 31906
706 323-9194

County Life
15 Roxbury Street
Keene, New Hampshire 03431
603 357-3975

County Life Buying Club
1917 Division Street
Nashville, Tennessee 37203
615 327-3695

County Life Natural Foods
PO Box 489
Pullman, Michigan 49450
269 236-5011

Country Life Store
211 N Lewis St
Glenville WV 26351
304 462-8157

Country Life
Independencia 584-B
Linares, 7 Region Chili
South America
56 73 22 1266

County Life
Melantrichova 15
11000 Prague 1 Czech Republic
420 2 2421 3366

County Life
Jungmannova 1
11000 Prague 1 Czech Republic
420 2 5704 4419

Country Life
#16-1 Nonhyun-Dong
Kangnam-Ku
Seoul 135-010 Korea
82 2 511 2402

Country Life
1-5-7 Hiyoshi-Cho
Maebashi City, Gumma-ken Japan
81 27 234 6724

Country Life
3-4 Warwick Street, London
UK W1R 5WA England
44 207 434 2922

Country Life
14 Rue Venture 1300
Marseille, France
33 4 96 11 2800

Country Life Health Food Store
Traugutta 34
Radom Poland
48 48 363 1568

Country Life
Aurel Filimon 16
Targu Mures 4300 Romania
40 265 16 88 22

Country Life
Sattelgasse 3 CH-4001
Basel Switzerland
41 61 261 09 39

Country Life
Box 100
Kiev-1 Ukraine
380 44 443 2404

WHOLESOME BREAKFASTS

CRUNCHY GRANOLA

4 c. regular oats
½ c. coconut
¾ c. slightly TOASTED
   PEANUTS or other nut
½ c. pumpkin or sunflower
   seeds (opt.)

¾ tsp. salt
3-4 Tbs. honey
1 Tbs. vanilla or maple flavoring
¼ c. oil
½ c. raisins or chopped dates

In bowl combine first five ingredients. In separate bowl mix together remaining liquid ingredients and add to dry. Mix together well with hands. Spread on cookie sheet. Bake at 300° for 20 minutes until lightly browned. Reduce temperature to 225° and continue baking until dry. Stir occasionally while baking. Remove from oven and add dried fruit.
YIELD: 6 c.

SIMPLE GRANOLA

1 c. water
½ c. oil
1½ c. pitted dates, packed into
   cup

1½ tsp. salt
2 Tbs. vanilla or maple flavoring
8 c. regular oats
1 c. chopped nuts or coconut

Blend together first five ingredients until creamy. In bowl put oats and nuts. Add blender contents and mix together well. Spread on cookie sheet. Bake at 300° for 20 minutes, until lightly browned. Reduce temperature to 225° and bake until dry and crisp (approx. 1-2 hrs.). Stir occasionally while baking.
YIELD: 11 c.

CASHEW-PINEAPPLE DELIGHT

6 c. quick oats
1 c. coconut (opt.)
½ c. chopped walnuts (opt.)
¾ c. cashew pieces
1 c. unsweetened pineapple
   juice

1 tsp. salt
1 Tbs. vanilla
2-4 Tbs. honey

Combine first three ingredients in bowl. Blend remaining ingredients until creamy and add to dry ingredients. Mix well with hands. Spread on cookie sheet and follow baking directions for CRUNCHY GRANOLA.
YIELD: 8 c.

WHOLESOME BREAKFASTS

BANANA-ORANGE GRANOLA

7 c. quick oats	2 Tbs. vanilla
1 c. coconut (opt.)	1½ Tbs. grated orange rind or
½ c. chopped nuts (opt.)	¼ tsp. orange extract
¼ c. orange juice concentrate	1¼ tsp. salt
1½ c. ripe bananas	1½ tsp. coriander
½ c. cashew pieces	2 Tbs. honey

In bowl combine first three ingredients. Blend remaining ingredients on high until creamy. Pour into dry ingredients and stir together. Spread on cookie sheet. Bake at 300° for 40 minutes, stirring after 20 minutes. Reduce temperature to 225° and bake until dry. Stir occasionally.

YIELD: 10 c.

BREAD CRUMB GRANOLA

6 c. whole grain BREAD CRUMBS	½ c. apple juice concentrate
1 c. coconut or chopped nuts	½ c. raisins or chopped dates

Combine first three ingredients in bowl and gently toss with hands. Place on cookie sheet and bake one hour at 300°, stirring every 15 minutes. Turn off heat and leave in oven to dry out. Then remove and add raisins. Store in airtight container. Simply delicious.

YIELD: 6 c.

Variation: May use other unsweetened fruit juice concentrate.

HOT APPLE GRANOLA

6 c. chopped apples	1 Tbs. coriander
¾ c. apple juice concentrate	3 c. GRANOLA of your choice
2 Tbs. cornstarch	

Cook apples in ½ c. of apple concentrate until soft. Mix remaining concentrate with cornstarch and coriander. Add to apples and cook until thick. Stir in granola just before serving.

YIELD: 5 c.

Note: Best to use granola that is not too sweet.

WHOLESOME BREAKFASTS

MEUSLI

1 c. regular or quick oats	1¼ c. SOY or NUT MILK
¾ c. grated apples	1-2 sliced bananas
¾ c. unsweetened pineapple or orange juice	2-3 Tbs. chopped walnuts or almonds (TOASTED are best)
1-2 chopped oranges	
¼ c. raisins or dates	

Lightly toast oats in the oven on a cookie sheet at 250° for 30-40 minutes. Grate apples into pineapple juice in bowl. Peel and chop oranges. Add to apples. Add oats and raisins. Stir together briefly. Cover bowl and soak overnight in refrigerator. Next day, add milk, sliced bananas and top with nuts.

YIELD: 6 c.

Variation: May replace milk and fruit juice with 2 c. pineapple or orange juice.

ALL BRAN

8 c. wheat bran	1¼ c. molasses (not blackstrap)
2 c. quick oats	1 c. warm water
1 tsp. salt	1 tsp. maple or vanilla flavoring

Mix together bran, oats and salt in bowl. In separate bowl, stir together molasses, water and flavoring well. Pour liquid ingredients into dry and toss with hands until well mixed. Spread ½ inch deep on lightly-oiled cookie sheet. Bake at 300° for 20 minutes, then at 225° until dry (approx. 1½ hours). Stir often. Serve with MILK of your choice and top with fresh fruit.

YIELD: 12 c.

WHOLESOME BREAKFASTS

COOKING TIME CHART FOR
WHOLE GRAIN CEREALS

GRAIN (1 cup)	WATER (in cups)	TIME
Barley, hulled, not pearled	4-5	2-3 hours
rolled or flaked	2	45-60 min.
Buckwheat groats	2	20-30 min.
Cornmeal	3-4	45-60 min.
Millet	3	45-60 min.
Oats, groats	5	2-3 hours
regular rolled	2-3	45-60 min.
quick	2	30-45 min.
Rice, brown	2-2½	45-60 min.
cream of rice	4	45 min.
(brown rice flour)		
Rye Berries	5	2-3 hours
flaked	2	45-60 min.
Wheat Berries	5	2-3 hours
cream of wheat	3	45-60 min.
cracked wheat	3	45-60 min.
flaked	2	45-60 min.

The amount of water often depends on whether you enjoy your cereal thick or creamy. When it is creamy, we often sprinkle granola on top — very tasty and chewy.

DIRECTIONS: Using a covered sauce pan bring salted water to a boil. Add cereal while stirring. Return to a boil, lower heat and simmer cereal for the recommended time. May use an asbestos pad to protect the bottom of pan and to slowly cook the grain. Do not stir whole grains unless you want them creamy and sticky. All grains may be lightly toasted (DEXTRINIZED) before cooking to enhance the flavor and reduce the cooking time.

SALT may be added to taste. Use ¼ to ¾ tsp. per cup of dry grain.

8

WHOLESOME BREAKFASTS

VARIOUS OTHER COOKING METHODS

1. OVERNIGHT METHOD: Using a covered sauce pan bring salted water to a boil. Add whole grains and simmer for one hour. Remove from heat and let sit overnight. In the morning bring to a boil again, simmer for 30 to 60 minutes until tender, or place in oven, covered, at 350° for one hour. This is good for wheat, rye and oat berries. This method should not be used in hot weather as the cereal may spoil overnight.

2. THERMOS METHOD: In the morning, combine 1 part grain with 2½ parts water, and salt and soak 8 hours. Drain soaking water into a saucepan, bring to a boil, add grain, bring to boil again. Pour hot water into a well insulated thermos to preheat. Drain. Add ingredients to thermos making sure there is enough liquid to fill bottle to neck. Screw top on firmly, lay bottle on side and leave for 8 hours. Serve in bowls with fruit or whip in blender with nut cream and/or dates.

3. CROCK POT: Place grain, hot water and salt in crock pot. Stir briefly to mix salt. For oat groats, millet, wheat and rye berries cook on high 1-2 hours then on low overnight. For all other cereals cook on low overnight. Use same amount of water as on the chart for cooking grains.

4. SPROUTED GRAIN CEREALS: To increase the nutritional value of cereals and to aid in their digestibility try sprouting grains before cooking them. They have a sweeter flavor because some of the starch has changed to sugar. Lightly steam sprouts until tender and serve with favorite nut milk and fruit.

5. OVEN METHOD: Place grain, water and salt in a casserole. Stir briefly to mix salt. Cover. Bake at 200° all night. Ready to serve in the morning.

BAKED OATMEAL

1-1½ c. chopped dates	5 c. SOY or NUT MILK
1¾ c. chopped fresh fruit of your choice	1 tsp. vanilla
	¾ tsp. salt
3 c. regular oats	1 c. coconut

Spread dates on bottom of 9" x 13" baking dish and cover dates with fruit. Layer oats on top of fruit. Stir together vanilla, salt and milk in bowl. Pour evenly and slowly over oats. Sprinkle with coconut. Bake 350° for 1 hour.
YIELD: 9" x 13" baking dish

WHOLESOME BREAKFASTS

JOHNNY'S CORN-MILLET PORRIDGE

5 c. water
½ c. millet
½ c. unrefined cornmeal

1 tsp. salt
½ c. coconut
½ c. chopped dates or raisins

Place first four ingredients in saucepan. Bring to boil and boil 2-3 minutes, stirring CONSTANTLY. Reduce heat. Cover and simmer 30 minutes, stirring occasionally. Then add last two ingredients. Stir together and pour into LECITHIN-OILED baking dish. Bake at 350° for 30 minutes.
YIELD: 6 c.
Variation: May add 1 c. diced apples.

CREAMY RICE PUDDING

2 c. COOKED BROWN RICE
1½ c. SOY or NUT MILK
½ c. chopped almonds or filberts
½ c. raisins
1 tsp. lemon juice
¼-½ tsp. grated lemon or orange rind

2 Tbs. honey or ¼ c. DATE BUTTER
¼ tsp. coriander
1 tsp. vanilla
⅛ tsp. salt
pinch of anise (optional)

Mix everything together. Pour into lightly oiled 8" x 8" baking dish. Bake at 350° for 45 minutes.
YIELD: 4 c.
Variation: 1. For creamier pudding add extra cup of milk and bake 10 more minutes. 2. May use other cooked whole grain cereals.

CAROB CEREAL PUDDING

1 c. uncooked brown rice or millet
3 c. water
4-6 Tbs. carob powder
¼ c. coconut (optional)

¾ c. pitted dates, packed into cup
1 Tbs. vanilla
¾ tsp. salt
2 tsp. coffee substitute

Continued on next page...

WHOLESOME BREAKFASTS

Soak rice or millet overnight in 2 c. water. In morning, drain off water. Blend soaked grain with 1 c. warm water on high speed until very creamy, 3-5 minutes. Add 2 c. water and remaining ingredients and blend well. Pour into saucepan and cook over medium heat until thick, stirring constantly with whisk. Put into oiled 8" x 8" baking dish. May top with chopped nuts. Bake at 350° for 45-60 minutes. Serve hot or cold with your favorite milk from the BEVERAGE section.

YIELD: 8" x 8" baking dish.

CREAM OF BUCKWHEAT

1 c. buckwheat groats	3-4 large ripe bananas
1 tsp. vanilla	unsweetened pineapple
1 tsp. salt	juice
6 c. SOY or NUT MILK	2 c. coarsely grated apples,
4 c. ground GRANOLA	packed into cup

Grind buckwheat groats in blender. Bring milk to boil in saucepan. Add ground buckwheat, salt and vanilla to milk, stirring constantly with whisk. Continue stirring, until thick.

Cover and reduce heat to low. Simmer ½ hour. Stir occasionally while simmering.

Grind your favorite granola in blender and then measure. Grate apples into pineapple juice to keep from turning brown. Likewise, slice bananas into a separate bowl with pineapple juice to cover.

Layer on bottom of 9" x 13" baking dish:
>2 c. ground granola (pat down)
>drained apples
>drained bananas
>cooked buckwheat
>remainder of ground granola

Cover with foil and baked at 350° for 45 minutes. May serve hot or cold.

WHOLESOME BREAKFASTS

COCONUT-CORNMEAL MOUNDS

2½ c. unrefined cornmeal	2¼ c. coconut
6 c. water	1¼ c. raisins
1 tsp. salt	½ c. orange juice concentrate

In small bowl mix together cornmeal and 2 c. of the water. Bring remainder of water and salt to boil. Slowly add cornmeal mixture while stirring. Bring to a boil again; reduce heat and cook slowly for 1½ hours. Best cooked in double boiler or with heat defractor. Refrigerate overnight. In morning, add 1¼ c. coconut and raisins, mixing in well with hands. With ⅓ c. (#12) ice cream scoop, make level mounds of cereal. Dip mounds first into orange juice concentrate, then into remaining coconut. Place on lightly-oiled or wax-papered cookie sheet. Bake at 350° for 45 minutes until browned. Serve with GRAPE SAUCE.

YIELD: 16-17 mounds

Variation: Dip in thawed apple juice concentrate and finely chopped nuts or STREUSEL TOPPING.

CREAM OF WHEAT

1 c. whole wheat berries	4-5 c. water
1 Tbs. oil	1 tsp. salt

DEXTRINIZE wheat berries in 300° oven for 45 minutes. May also toast in dry skillet until nutty aroma rises. Grind in seed mill or blender until fine. Add oil and ground wheat to skillet and saute, stirring together while cooking. Add water and bring to boil. Reduce heat and simmer 30-40 minutes. Wonderful homemade flavor.

YIELD: 5 c.

Variation: May use any whole grain.

MILLET CRUMBLE

1 c. millet	1½ tsp. salt
3 c. water	1½ tsp. grated lemon rind (opt.)
3 c. unsweetened pineapple juice	4 c. GRANOLA
3 tsp. vanilla	4 c. sliced bananas

Continued on next page...

WHOLESOME BREAKFASTS

In saucepan bring water and millet to boil; cover and simmer 45-60 minutes. Place 2 c. granola on bottom of lightly-oiled 9" x 13" baking dish. Layer bananas on top of granola. When millet is done, blend on high speed until creamy: 1 c. hot, cooked millet, 1 c. pineapple juice, 1 tsp. vanilla, ½ tsp. salt, and ½ tsp. grated lemon rind. Pour over bananas. Repeat procedure two or more times. Top with remaining 2 c. granola. Serve immediately for a soft crumble or chill for a firm crumble.

YIELD: 9" x 13" baking dish

Variation: Add ¼ c. coconut to millet while blending.

BREAKFAST BANANA SPILT

Using an ice cream scoop, place 3 mounds of cooked cereal (millet, rice, oatmeal, etc.) into banana split dish or bowl. Cut peeled banana lengthwise and dip into unsweetened pineapple juice. Place each half on either side of cereal mounds. Top two of the mounds with thickened fruit toppings such as STRAWBERRY or BLUEBERRY. Cover the third mound with CAROB "HOT FUDGE" TOPPING. Place a dollop of SOY WHIPPED CREAM on each mound and sprinkle with chopped nuts. A delightful way to teach children to enjoy whole grain cereals.

TASTY POPCORN

Contrary to popular opinion, popcorn makes a nutritious and tasty breakfast dish. It is an excellent source of dietary fiber and complex carbohydrate as well as a good source of protein: 1.8 g/cup popped.

May be eaten dry or as a cereal with milk or fruit juice. Yeast flakes or COUNTRY-STYLE SEASONING give it a savory, cheesy flavor.

Air popping is very popular and avoids the added calories and digestive difficulties of oil-popped popcorn, as well as the possible formation of harmful chemicals caused by overheating vegetable oils.

To flavor air-popped popcorn: pop ½ dry popcorn. Dribble 1-2 Tbs. oil (olive is best) or 1-2 Tbs. tahini on top. Then sprinkle with salt, yeast flakes or COUNTRY-STYLE SEASONING to taste. To revive leftover popcorn, put in 250° over 20-30 minutes.

WHOLESOME BREAKFASTS

APPLE-OATMEAL BREAKFAST BARS

1 c. shredded raw apples,
    packed into cup
1 tsp. grated orange or
    lemon rind
1½ c. regular oats
2 Tbs. oil

¾ c. water
½ tsp. salt
¾ c. chopped dates
¼ c. chopped nuts
1½ tsp. vanilla

Blend ¾ c. oats on high to make oat flour. Pour into bowl and add remaining ingredients. Stir together well. Press evenly to LECITHIN-OILED 8" x 8" baking dish. Bake at 375° for 20-25 minutes. When cool, cut into bars.
YIELD: 16 - 2" x 2" bars

FRUITY RICE SQUARES

2 c. brown rice
2 c. coconut
1 tsp. salt
2 tsp. vanilla

¼ c. tahini or peanut butter
½ c. apple juice concentrate or
    ¼ c. honey & 2 Tbs. water

Blend 1 c. dry rice on high speed for 30 seconds. Stop blender and stir contents. Repeat procedure two more times. Add 1 c. coconut to blended rice and blend together for 15-20 seconds more. Empty contents into bowl. Repeat steps again using second cup of rice and coconut. Mix all ingredients together well. Firmly press half evenly into lightly oiled 8" x 8" baking dish. Spread 1 c. OF DATE BUTTER or favorite DRIED FRUIT BUTTER on top. Crumble remaining half on top of DATE BUTTER and press down lightly. Bake at 350° for 40 minutes.
YIELD: 16 - 2" x 2" squares

FRUIT LASAGNE

2 c. mashed tofu
½ tsp. salt
6 c. chopped fruit, fresh or
    canned
1½ c. unsweetened fruit juice

2½ c. DRIED FRUIT BUTTER
1½ c. chopped nuts
1 lb. uncooked soy or whole
    wheat lasagne noodles

Continued on next page...

WHOLESOME BREAKFASTS

Rinse, drain and mash tofu. In bowl combine tofu and salt. In another bowl, mix together fruit, juice and DRIED FRUIT BUTTER.

Layer in 9" x 13" lightly-oiled baking dish:
1. 2½ c. fruit mixture
2. lasagne noodles
3. 1 c. tofu
4. ½ c. nuts
5. 2 c. fruit mixture
Repeat #2-5

Garnish with nuts. Bake at 350° for 60 minutes, until noodles are tender.

Suggested combinations:
pears and DATE BUTTER,
crushed pineapple and APRICOT BUTTER,
peaches and DATE BUTTER,
apples and PRUNE BUTTER
YIELD: 9" x 13" baking dish

APPLE BREAD-FEST

2 Tbs. lemon juice
4 c. sliced apples
6 c. ½" bread cubes
½ c. wheat germ or ground GRANOLA
1½ c. apple juice concentrate (12 oz.)

½ tsp. salt
1 tsp. vanilla
½ c. TOASTED PEANUTS or other nut
½ c. raisins

Slice apples into lemon juice and mix in bowl to coat apples. Add remaining ingredients. Stir together carefully in order not to break bread cubes. Spoon into lightly oiled 9" x 13" baking dish. Do not pack. Bake at 400° for 30 minutes. Serve hot with milk from the BEVERAGE section.
YIELD: 9" x 13" baking dish
Note: To make ground granola, blend until fine.

WHOLESOME BREAKFASTS

OLD FASHIONED BREAD PUDDING

6 c. 1" whole grain bread cubes

½ c. coarsely chopped walnuts

1 c. chopped apples

1 recipe SWEET CASHEW MILK

Mix all ingredients together carefully in a bowl. Pour into LECITHIN-OILED 8" x 8" baking dish. Bake at 350° for 45 minutes.

YIELD: 8 c. or 8" x 8" baking dish

APPLE BROWN BETTY

10 c. sliced or diced apples (3 lbs.)

½ c. raisins or currants

1 tsp. CINNAMON SUBSTITUTE

½ c. honey or 2 Tbs. honey and ⅓ apple juice concentrate

5-6 c. ½" whole grain bread cubes

1 c. unsweetened pineapple juice

1 recipe LEMON SAUCE

Wash and core apples. Slice or dice unpeeled apples into 9" x 13" baking dish. Sprinkle raisins and cinnamon substitute over apples. Drizzle with honey. Cover apples with cubed bread. Drizzle pineapple juice over bread, soaking it as much as possible. Cover with foil and bake at 350° for 45-60 minutes or until apples are tender. Remove from oven and top with LEMON SAUCE. May serve hot or cover with saran wrap and chill. Delicious served with SOY WHIPPED CREAM or NUT MILK.

YIELD: 9" x 13" baking dish.

LAYERED BREAD PUDDING

12 slices whole grain bread

2½ c. SOY or NUT MILK or unsweetened fruit juice

3½ c. fresh or canned chopped fruit

2 c. DRIED FRUIT BUTTER

1¾ c. chopped nuts

Continued on next page...

WHOLESOME BREAKFASTS

If using fresh fruit, briefly cook to soften in small amount of water. Cover bottom of 9" x 13" baking dish with one layer of bread (approx. 6 slices). Moisten bread with half the milk or juice. Cover bread with fruit, then ¾ c. chopped nuts. Add another layer of bread and moisten with remaining milk or juice. Spread fruit butter on top. Sprinkle on remaining nuts. Bake at 350° for 30 - 45 minutes. Delicious hot or cold with milk from the BEVERAGE section.

Suggested combinations:
1. Apples and DATE BUTTER or PRUNE BUTTER.
2. Pears and DATE BUTTER or FIG BUTTER.
3. Peaches and FAVORITE APRICOT BUTTER or DATE BUTTER

YIELD: 9" x 13" baking dish

GRANOLA CRISP TOPPING

½ c. **DATE BUTTER or** ¼ c. **honey**	1 tsp. coriander
	1 tsp. vanilla
3 Tbs. oil	3 c. regular oats
2 Tbs. water	½ c. chopped nuts or coconut
½ tsp. salt	

Stir together ingredients in bowl. Mix well with hands. Crumble over fruit filling of your choice in 8" x 8" baking dish. Bake at 350° for 45 minutes or until golden.
YIELD: 3 c.

CRUMBLE TOPPING

3 c. regular oats	¾ tsp. salt
1½ c. coconut	3 Tbs. honey
1½ tsp. coriander	3 Tbs. water

Blend half the oats and half the coconut together until finely ground. Empty into mixing bowl. Repeat. Add remaining ingredients and mix together well with hands. Crumble over fruit-filling of your choice in 8" x 8" baking dish. Bake at 350° for 45 minutes or until golden.
YIELD: 4 c.

WHOLESOME BREAKFASTS

CRUMB CRISP TOPPING

2 c. regular oats	2 Tbs. oil
1 c. coconut	3 Tbs. water
1 c. quick oats	¼ c. honey
½ c. chopped nuts	1 tsp. vanilla
¾ tsp. salt	1 tsp. coriander

Finely grind together first two ingredients, half at a time, in blender 15-20 seconds, emptying blender into mixing bowl. Add next three ingredients. Mix together well. In another bowl, beat together last five ingredients. Add to dry ingredients and mix together well. Crumble topping over fruit-filling of your choice in 8″ x 8″ baking dish. Bake at 325° for 45 minutes or until golden.

YIELD: 4 c.

BREAKFAST BANANA CRISP

3 c. CRISP or CRUMBLE TOPPING	⅛ tsp. salt
3 c. sliced bananas	½ c. pitted dates, packed into cup
¼ c. water	1¼ c. ripe, mashed bananas (approx. 2 large)
2 Tbs. lemon juice	

Put 1½ c. of CRISP or CRUMBLE TOPPING on bottom of 8″ x 8″ baking dish. Cover with sliced bananas. Blend remaining ingredients for about 45 seconds. Pour over sliced bananas. Sprinkle with remainder of topping.

Bake at 350° for 45 minutes or until golden brown. Serve hot or cold with SOY or NUT MILK.

YIELD: 8″ x 8″ baking dish

BEST CORN-OAT WAFFLES

7 c. regular oats	2 tsp. salt
8-9 c. water	½ c. dates or ¼ c. honey
1 c. unrefined cornmeal	2 Tbs. vanilla or maple extract
¼ c. oil	

Stir all ingredients together in bowl. Blend 3 c. of batter at a time for 15 seconds and pour into another bowl. Repeat procedure until all batter is blended.

Continued on next page...

WHOLESOME BREAKFASTS

DIRECTIONS FOR BAKING: Prepare waffle iron by brushing lightly with LECITHIN-OIL mixture. Close lid and preheat on high 5-8 minutes. When waffle iron is hot, sprinkle sesame seeds on bottom for easy removal and enhanced flavor. Pour 1¾ c. batter over seeds and sprinkle more seeds on top of batter. Close lid and bake 10-12 minutes. Cool waffle. Before freezing or stacking place saran wrap or waxed paper between waffle.
YIELD: 6 - 9" x 9" waffles

CAROB WAFFLES

3 c. warm water
1½ c. regular oats
½ c. coconut
½ c. carob powder
¾ tsp. salt

2 tsp. vanilla
½ tsp. coffee substitute
8 pitted dates or 2-3 Tbs. honey

Blend all ingredients on high 1-2 minutes until creamy. Pour into bowl and let stand 10-15 minutes to allow to thicken. Follow cooking directions for BEST CORN—OAT WAFFLES. Elegantly delicious served with STRAWBERRY SAUCE and SOY WHIPPED CREAM.
YIELD: 2 - 9" x 9" waffles

BREAD WAFFLES

2 c. water
1 c. regular oats
3 slices whole grain bread
2 tsp. vanilla or maple flavoring

¼ tsp. salt
2 Tbs. honey or ¼ c. DATE BUTTER
2 Tbs. oil (optional)

Cut bread into 5-6 pieces. Put in blender and blend ingredients together. Bake 8-10 minutes in LECITHIN-OILED, preheated waffle iron. A good way to use old bread.
YIELD: 2 - 9" x 9" waffles
Note: when using savory bread (onion, dill, rye), omit honey and vanilla and add onion and/or garlic powder to taste.

WHOLESOME BREAKFASTS

—————— AUNT MAY'S VERY LIGHT WAFFLES ——————

2½ c. water or SOY MILK
2 c. regular oats
2 Tbs. sesame seeds
2 Tbs. whole grain flour
2 tsp. liquid or granular lecithin

¾ tsp. salt
2 tsp. vanilla, maple or lemon extract
2 Tbs. honey or 3 Tbs. apple juice concentrate or ¼ c. raisins or dates

Blend all ingredients until creamy. Pour batter into bowl. Follow cooking directions for BEST CORN-OAT WAFFLES.
YIELD: 2 - 9" x 9" waffles

——————— SOY-OAT WAFFLES or PANCAKES ———————

1 c. SOAKED SOYBEANS
1⅔ c. water
2-4 Tbs. apple juice concentrate
1¼ c. regular oats

2 Tbs. oil (optional)
½ tsp. salt
2 tsp. vanilla or maple flavoring

Blend all ingredients together well. Use batter as soon as possible so bean taste will not get strong. Bake waffles 12-15 minutes in hot waffle iron following directions for BEST CORN-OAT WAFFLES or make pancakes on hot griddle.
YIELD: 2 - 9" x 9" waffles or 12 - ¼ c. pancakes
Variation: May use 2 c. water and 6-8 pitted dates in place of 1⅔ c. water and apple juice.

——————————— RICE WAFFLES ———————————

2 c. cooked rice

Evenly press rice onto hot LECITHIN-OILED waffle iron with spoon. To keep rice from sticking to spoon, dip into water. Press top of waffle iron firmly to rice. Bake on high for 15-20 minutes or until golden brown.
YIELD: 1 - 9" x 9" waffle
Variations:
1. May use other cooked whole grain cereals.
2. May add dried fruit, nuts or seeds to cooked cereal before baking.
3. For savory flavor, sprinkle with onion or garlic powder, COUNTRY-STYLE SEASONING, salt or herbs to taste.

WHOLESOME BREAKFASTS

HASHBROWN WAFFLES

4 c. shredded raw potatoes
2 Tbs. oil (olive is best)
　(optional)
2-3 tsp. onion powder
¼-½ tsp. garlic powder

1 tsp. salt
4 tsp. yeast flakes (optional)
2 Tbs. dried parsley

Mix all ingredients together well. Press into pre-heated, LECITHIN-OILED waffle iron. Close lid firmly and bake 12-15 minutes until browned. Delicious with KETCHUP and SCRAMBLED TOFU.

YIELD: 2 - 9" x 9" waffles

Variation: Recipe works well with leftover cooked potatoes peeled.

CREPE SUZETTES

2 c. whole wheat flour
2 c. regular oats
¾ tsp. salt
4 c. water or SOY MILK

2 Tbs. oil
2 Tbs. honey
1 Tbs. vanilla or maple flavoring

Mix ingredients together in bowl. Blend 2 c. of batter at a time until smooth and empty into another bowl. Repeat until all of batter is blended.

DIRECTIONS FOR COOKING: Lightly LECITHIN-OIL skillet and heat on medium-high. When hot, pour ⅓ c. of batter onto skillet. Quickly spread with bottom of measuring cup. When edges are cooked and bottom is golden, turn to brown on other side.

TO SERVE: Place STRAWBERRY or BLUEBERRY TOPPING in center of crepes and roll up. Top with SOY or TOFU WHIPPED CREAM.

YIELD: 18 Crepes

Note: Non-stick pans work the best.

YUMMY PANCAKES

Use ingredients and cooking directions for CREPE SUZETTES with the following exceptions. Use ¼ c. portions of batter. Do not spread. When edges of pancakes are cooked and bottom is golden, turn to brown on other side.

Delicious topped with APPLE SYRUP.

YIELD: 25 - ¼ c. pancakes

WHOLESOME BREAKFASTS

GERMAN BLINTZES

Fill CREPE SUZETTES with PINEAPPLE TOFU COTTAGE CHEESE and roll together. Cover with STRAWBERRY TOPPING and a dollop of SOY or TOFU WHIPPED CREAM.

CASHEW FRENCH TOAST

1¾ c. water	¾ c. cashew pieces
8 pitted dates	8 slices whole grain bread
⅛ tsp. salt	

Bring dates and water to boil in saucepan. Remove from heat and let sit for 5 minutes. Add to blender with remaining ingredients. Blend on high until creamy. Pour batter into pie pan or shallow baking dish. Coat both sides of bread with batter. Place on LECITHIN-OILED cookie sheet. Broil 7-10 minutes on each side until brown. Watch carefully. May also bake at 400° for 15 minutes on each side.

YIELD: Approx. 8 slices french toast

FLAXSEED FRENCH TOAST

1 c. cashew pieces or soy flour	¾ tsp. salt
3 c. warm water	1 Tbs. lecithin
2 Tbs. cornstarch	1 Tbs. oil
¼ c. flaxseed	3 Tbs. honey
1 Tbs. vanilla	¼ tsp. coriander
	12 slices whole grain bread

WHEN USING CASHEWS: Blend 1 c. water and cashews on high speed 1-2 minutes until creamy. Add 1 more cup water and remaining ingredients (except bread). Blend on high speed until flax thickens mixture. Add remaining cup of water and continue blending until thick again.

WHEN USING SOY FLOUR: Blend 2 c. water, soy flour and remaining ingredients (except bread) on high speed until flax thickens mixture. Add remaining cup of water and continue blending until thick again.

Pour into bowl and dip bread into batter until well soaked. Place close together on LECITHIN-OILED cookie sheet. Bake at 400° about 15 minutes or until light brown on bottom. Turn and bake 5-10 minutes more.

YIELD: 12 slices french toast

Note: These are delicious when done.

WHOLESOME BREAKFASTS

SPOON BREAD

2 c. hot water	1 tsp. onion powder
4 c. frozen corn	1 c. unrefined cornmeal
1 tsp. salt	

Blend first four ingredients on high until creamy. Stop blender and add cornmeal. Stir contents before blending. Briefly blend again. Pour into LECITHIN-OILED 8" x 8" baking dish and bake at 400° for 45-60 minutes until golden brown.
YIELD: 8" x 8" baking dish

Variations:
1. Corn Waffles: Bake 15-20 minutes in LECITHIN-OILED waffle iron. Set on high.
YIELD: 3 - 9" x 9" waffles

2. Corn Crispies: Using grill side of waffle iron, pour ½ c. batter on hot grill. Spread to 6" circle with bottom of measuring cup. Let sit on open grill one minute before closing lid. Bake 7 minutes or until golden.
YIELD: 10 - 6" corn crispies

3. Corn Pancakes: Follow procedure for corn crispies using LECITHIN-OILED cookie sheet and baking at 400° for 15 minutes until brown. Flip and bake another 3-4 minutes.
YIELD: 10 - 6" pancakes

4. May add 1 c. drained, chopped kale to all of the above recipes for a nutritious and delicious addition.

WHOLESOME BREAKFASTS

STRAWBERRY TOPPING

4 c. whole unsweetened
frozen strawberries
¾ c. apple juice concentrate

¹⁄₁₆ tsp. salt
3 Tbs. cornstarch

Place berries in bowl and thaw overnight at room temperature. Next day drain and save juice. Pour into blender and add remaining ingredients. Briefly blend on high. Pour into sauce pan and bring to boil stirring constantly until thick and clear. Be careful not to scorch. Remove from heat. Add berries and gently fold together with rubber spatula. Chill.

YIELD: 3 c.

Note: To use as a filling, add 1 Tbs. more cornstarch.

Variation: Use ½ c. apple juice concentrate and ¼ c. grape juice concentrate in place of ¾ c. apple juice concentrate.

BLUEBERRY TOPPING

4 c. frozen blueberries
½ c. RUNNY DATE BUTTER
(optional)

¹⁄₁₆ tsp. salt
½ c. apple juice concentrate
3 Tbs. cornstarch

Put first three ingredients in saucepan and boil, stirring frequently, until berries give off juice. Blend or whisk together cornstarch and apple concentrate. Add to boiling berries while stirring and cook until clear. Stir and cook one more minute. As berries cook color will deepen.

YIELD: 3 c.

Note: To use as a filling add 1 Tbs. more cornstarch.

APPLE-DATE TOPPING

8 c. sliced apples
1 c. unsweetened pineapple
juice
1 c. pitted dates

⅛ tsp. salt
¾ tsp. coriander
⅛ tsp. anise (optional)

Continued on next page...

Put all ingredients into saucepan and cook over medium heat until apples are soft. Stir occasionally.

YIELD: 5 c.

PEACH-RAISIN TOPPING

4½ c. sliced fresh or canned peaches
¾ c. peach liquid or unsweetened pineapple juice
1 Tbs. vanilla
⅛ tsp. salt
½ c. raisins
¾ c. apple juice concentrate
3½ Tbs. cornstarch

Put first five ingredients into saucepan and cook over medium heat until raisins are soft. Stir occasionally. Mix apple juice concentrate and cornstarch together with fork. Add to hot fruit while stirring. Cook until clear and thickened.

YIELD: 5½ c.

Note: When using canned peaches drain liquid.

CAROB-BANANA TOFU TOPPING

1 c. sliced bananas
1 c. tofu
2 Tbs. honey or ½ c. RUNNY DATE BUTTER
3-4 Tbs. carob powder
¼ tsp. salt
1 Tbs. vanilla
½ c. SOY OR NUT MILK
¼ tsp. coffee substitute

Rinse and drain tofu. Crumble with hands and measure. Put tofu into blender. Add remaining ingredients and blend on high until creamy, stopping blender several times to stir contents. Keep refrigerated.

YIELD: 3 c.

CAROB "HOT FUDGE" TOPPING

2 c. water
1 c. cashew pieces
4-6 Tbs. carob powder
1½ c. pitted dates (about 35)
½ tsp. salt
½ tsp. coffee substitute
2 tsp. vanilla

Continued on next page...

Soak dates in 1 c. hot water. Blend remaining cup of water and cashews on high until creamy 1-2 minutes. Stop blender; add remaining ingredients, dates and water. Blend until creamy 2-3 minutes, stopping blender 3 or 4 times to stir contents. Pour into saucepan and cook over medium-high until thick, stirring constantly. Serve hot or cold.
YIELD: 2½ c.

FUDGY CAROB SYRUP

1 c. CAROB "HOT FUDGE" TOPPING   ½ c. water

Stir together well. Delicious served over cooked cereals, WAFFLES or FRENCH TOAST.
YIELD: 1¼ c.

APPLE SYRUP

6 oz. can frozen apple juice concentrate (¾ c.)
¾ c. water (fill apple concentrate can)
4 tsp. cornstarch, level
½ tsp. lemon juice
¼ tsp. coriander

Blend all ingredients briefly on high. Pour into saucepan and cook over medium stirring constantly until thickened and clear. Keep refrigerated.
YIELD: 1½ c.

ORANGE-DATE SYRUP

3 c. unsweetened orange juice
1 c. pitted dates, packed into cup
¼ tsp. vanilla
⅛ tsp. salt

Blend 2 c. orange juice with rest of ingredients on high speed until creamy. Add remaining cup of orange juice and blend briefly.
YIELD: 3½ c.
Variation: May replace last cup of orange juice with water for a milder orange flavor.

WHOLESOME BREAKFASTS

─── ALMOND CREAM FRUIT DRESSING ───

1 c. unsweetened pineapple
or apple juice
¼-½ c. almonds (BLANCHED
is best)

1 tsp. honey or 2-3 tsp. DATE
BUTTER
⅛ tsp. salt

Blend ingredients on high until creamy – 2 minutes. Delicious on APPLE
WALDORF SALAD or any fresh fruit salad.
YIELD: 1½ c.

─── CHOCK-FULL-O-NUTS CREAM ───

1 c. water
½-1 c. raw nuts of your choice
extract

2 Tbs. honey or 6-8 pitted dates
⅛ tsp. salt

Blend all ingredients together on high speed until creamy, 1-2 minutes.
Suggested combinations:
1. cashew or brazil nuts and 1 tsp. vanilla extract
2. filberts and ¼ tsp. almond extract
3. almonds and ¼ tsp. almond extract
4. walnuts or pecans and 1 tsp. maple extract
Delicious served over FRUIT CRISP, BREAD PUDDING or fruit salad.
YIELD: 1½ c.

─── SUMMER FRUIT CREAM ───

1 c. cashew pieces
1 c. unsweetened pineapple
juice

3 Tbs. apple juice concentrate
⅛ tsp. salt
¼ tsp. lemon juice

Blend all ingredients on high 1-2 minutes until creamy. Serve over fruit
salad as is or may thicken. Pour into saucepan and cook on medium-high
until thick, stirring constantly. Then chill and spread on APPLE
AMBROSIA PIE.
YIELD: 1¾ c. uncooked, 1⅓ c. cooked

WHOLESOME BREAKFASTS

GRAPE SAUCE

Using GRAPE JAM recipe, blend grape juice, raisins and salt. Place in saucepan. Add ¼ c. minute tapioca and let sit for 10 minutes. Bring to a boil; reduce heat and simmer until tapioca is clear, stirring constantly.
YIELD: 2 c.

SIMPLE FRESH FRUIT FILLING

6 c. fresh sliced fruit of your choice

1 c. unsweetened pineapple or apple juice

Place fruit in 8″ x 8″ baking dish and pour juice over it. Cover with 3-4 c. TOPPING of your choice. Bake at 350° for 30-45 minutes or until golden brown. Delicious served with milk from the BEVERAGE section.
YIELD: 8″ x 8″ baking dish

BANANA-PEANUT TREAT

½ c. unsweetened pineapple juice
¼ c. peanut butter
¼ tsp. salt

5 large, ripe bananas
½ c. TOASTED unsalted peanuts

In bowl beat together first three ingredients with whisk or fork until creamy. Slice bananas into mixture. Add peanuts. Gently fold together. Delicious on FRENCH TOAST, WAFFLES, in CREPES – even on cereal.
YIELD: 3 c.

TOFU-PINEAPPLE "COTTAGE CHEESE"

2 c. mashed tofu
1½ c. unsweetened crushed pineapple
½ tsp. salt
½ c. chopped, TOASTED nuts (optional) (do not use walnuts or pecans; they turn tofu purplish)

½ c. SOY WHIPPED CREAM
or
3 Tbs. honey
½ c. mashed tofu
1 Tbs. oil
1 tsp. vanilla

Continued on next page...

Rinse tofu and squeeze out excess water with hands. Mash with fork or potato masher and then measure tofu. Place in bowl. Add remaining ingredients and mix together well. In place of WHIPPED CREAM may use last four ingredients blended together until creamy. Serve with fruit salad or in CREPES. Delightful on pineapple ring topped with strawberry.
YIELD: 4 c.

DATE BUTTER

1 c. pitted dates   **¾ c. warm water**

Put ingredients into saucepan and bring to boil. Remove from heat and let sit for 5 minutes. Then blend on high until smooth. May also soak dates in hot water for 15 minutes and then blend until smooth.

To have on hand for use in cookies, cakes, pies or granola, make a large batch and freeze in pint or quart containers.

Delicious on toast, muffins, WAFFLES, etc.

YIELD: 1¼ c.

Variations: May use other dried fruits. When using figs, apricots, prunes it is easier to blend if fruit is first cut into pieces before putting into water.

RUNNY DATE BUTTER

2 c. pitted dates   **2 c. warm water**

Follow directions for DATE BUTTER.
YIELD: 2½ c.

DRIED FRUIT BUTTER

1 c. dried fruit   **¾-1 c. warm water**

Follow directions for DATE BUTTER. When using figs, apricots, prunes it is easier to blend if fruit is first cut into pieces before putting into water.

WHOLESOME BREAKFASTS

—— FAVORITE APRICOT BUTTER ——

1½ c. unsweetened pineapple
juice or water
1 c. pitted dates

1 c. dried, sulphured apricots,
cut in half
1-3 tsp. lemon juice (optional)

Follow directions for DATE BUTTER.
YIELD: 2 c.
Variation: Use apricots in place of dates for a rich apricot flavor.

—— PINEAPPLE-APRICOT BUTTER ——

Prepare FAVORITE APRICOT BUTTER and add 1 c. crushed pineapple. A refreshing spread.
YIELD: 3 c.

—— APPLE BUTTER ——

2½ c. hot apple juice or water
1½ c. dried apples, packed
into cup

⅛ tsp. salt
¾ tsp. coriander
1 Tbs. lemon juice

Place first two ingredients in bowl and soak for 15 minutes. Pour into blender and add remaining ingredients. Blend on high until smooth, stopping blender 2-3 times to stir contents.
YIELD: 3 c.

—— FESTIVE FRUIT BUTTER ——

Make APPLE BUTTER recipe substituting grape juice for apple juice. Omit coriander and lemon juice. Add ½ tsp. grated orange or lemon rind.
YIELD: 3 c.

—— ORANGE FIG BUTTER ——

1¼ c. calimyrna figs (13)
1 c. unsweetened orange juice

½ c. water

Continued on next page...

WHOLESOME BREAKFASTS

Cut ends of stems off figs and cut in half. Put figs in saucepan with remaining ingredients. Bring to boil. Remove from heat and let sit 5 minutes. Then blend on high until smooth, stopping blender once or twice to stir contents.
YIELD: 2 c.

GRAPE JAM

2 c. unsweetened grape juice   3 Tbs. + 1 tsp. cornstarch
1 c. raisins   pinch salt

Blend all ingredients on high until smooth. Pour into saucepan and cook over medium-high heat stirring constantly, until thick and clear. Pour into covered jar or container. Delicious on toast or muffins.
YIELD: 2¼ c.
Variations: May use unsweetened pineapple juice and dried pineapple.

GRAPE JELLY

1 c. unsweetened grape juice   4 tsp. agar-agar flakes

Combine ingredients in a saucepan. Let sit 2 minutes. Bring to boil. Reduce heat and simmer 1 minute or until agar is dissolved, stirring frequently. Pour into container and cover to chill. Keep refrigerated.
YIELD: 1 c.

ORANGE-APRICOT MARMALADE

1 c. orange juice   ¼ c. honey
¼ c. pineapple juice   ¼-⅓ c. finely chopped, dried
2 Tbs. orange juice concentrate   apricots (sulphured)
2 Tbs. grated orange rind   3 Tbs. GROUND TAPIOCA

Put all ingredients into saucepan and stir together. Heat on low, stirring occasionally. Be careful not to scorch. Keep covered when not stirring. When tapioca is clear pour into container, cover and chill.
YIELD: 2 c.

WHOLESOME BREAKFASTS

CAROB-TAHINI SPREAD

1 c. water
1 Tbs. vanilla
7 Tbs. carob powder
⅔ c. pitted dates, packed into cup

½ tsp. salt (¼ tsp. if using salted peanut butter)
1 tsp. coffee substitute
¾ c. tahini, peanut or almond butter

Place all ingredients in blender except nut butter and blend until creamy. Add nut butter of your choice and continue to blend until well mixed. Store in refrigerator. Makes a delicious cake or muffin icing.
YIELD: 2¼ c.

CASHEW FRUIT SPREAD

1 c. cashew pieces
½ c. apple juice concentrate
pinch salt (optional)

⅓ c. finely chopped dried apricots or other dried fruit

Blend all ingredients except apricots on high speed until smooth (1-2 minutes). Remove from blender and stir in apricots. Keep refrigerated.
YIELD: 1¼ c.

TAHINI DATE SPREAD

⅔ c. DATE BUTTER
¼ c. tahini or sesame butter

¼ c. water
2 Tbs. sunflower seeds

Mix ingredients together well until creamy. Store in refrigerator.
YIELD: 1 c.

SUNNY SESAME TREAT

½ c. peanut butter
½ c. tahini or sesame butter

¼ c. honey

Mix ingredients together until creamy. Delicious on toast topped with bananas or raisins.
YIELD: one heaping cup

WHOLESOME BREAKFASTS

"If you can get apples, you are in a good condition as far as fruit is concerned, if you have nothing else . . . Apples are superior to any fruit for a stand by that grows."

Ellen G. White

COUNSELS ON DIET AND FOODS, p. 312

Here are some of our favorite ways to prepare apples that tell your family & friends — "I love you".

FRESH STUFFED APPLE

Core an apple. Stuff center with either peanut butter and dates or SPREAD of your choice. Serve.

A real child-pleaser.

Variation: May also use pears.

BAKED APPLES

4 medium apples
¼ c. orange or apple juice concentrate
¼ c. chopped nuts

¼ c. DATE BUTTER or raisins
½ c. whole wheat BREAD CRUMBS
2 tsp. vanilla

Wash and core apples. Mix remaining ingredients together in small bowl and stuff center of each apple. Place in 8″ x 8″ baking dish filled with 1 c. water or fruit juice. Cover with foil and bake at 350° for 1 hour or until soft.
YIELD: 4 baked apples

APPLE DUMPLINGS

4 apples

Make one recipe of BAKED APPLES, without baking them and one recipe of FLAKY WHEAT-OAT PIE CRUST. Divide pie dough into quarters and roll each piece into a circle. Place one apple in the center of each circle. Cover each apple with dough except for hole at top. Place covered apples in 8″ x 8″ baking dish. Do not add 1 c. water or juice to bottom of pan as in BAKED APPLES. Bake at 350° for 1 hour.
YIELD: 4 apple dumplings

WHOLESOME BREAKFASTS

APPLE WALDORF SALAD

5 c. diced fresh apples
1 c. raisins or chopped dates

½ c. coarsely chopped walnuts
(TOASTED is best)

Chop apples and put into unsweetened pineapple juice to prevent discoloration. Drain apples and combine all ingredients. Dress with one recipe of ALMOND FRUIT CREAM or SUMMER FRUIT CREAM. May also use fresh-squeezed lemon juice and honey to taste and/or pineapple juice.
YIELD: 6 c.

APPLE AMBROSIA PIE

2 c. apple juice
3½ Tbs. GROUND TAPIOCA
2 c. finely shredded red apples

½ tsp. coriander
⅛ tsp. salt (optional)
¼-½ c. finely chopped, TOASTED nuts

In a saucepan, soak tapioca in apple juice for 30-45 minutes. Cook over medium heat until clear, stirring constantly. Remove from heat. Shred apples; measure and add to tapioca with coriander and salt. Mix together and spread into baked COCONUT-OAT pie shell. Chill. Before serving ice with 1 c. of SUMMER FRUIT CREAM and sprinkle nuts on top.
YIELD: 1 level 9" pie.

JENNIFER'S RAISIN BRAN MUFFINS

2½ c. warm water
⅓ c. oil
2 c. regular oats
1 c. raisins
2 Tbs. baking yeast
⅓ c. honey
2¼ c. whole wheat flour

1½ c. wheat bran
2 tsp. salt
1 Tbs. vanilla
¼ c. molasses
2 tsp. lemon extract or 1 Tbs. grated lemon rind

Combine 1½ c. water, oil, oats, and raisin in mixing bowl. Let stand 5 minutes. Mix together in small bowl 1 cup water, yeast and 1 Tbs. honey. While the yeast bubbles, add remaining ingredients to raisin-oat mixture and stir together. Add yeast mixture and mix again. Scoop into LECITHIN-OILED muffin tins. Bake at 375° for 10 minutes; reduce heat to 350° and continue baking for 20-30 minutes more.
YIELD: 12 - ½ c. muffins or 18 - ⅓ c. muffins

WHOLESOME BREAKFASTS

BREAKFAST BRAN MUFFINS

3 c. warm water
½ c. molasses
¼ c. oil
2-4 Tbs. liquid lecithin
1½ tsp. salt
1½ c. raisins
1 Tbs. baking yeast

1 c. oat bran
1 c. wheat bran
1½ c. whole wheat flour
1 c. whole wheat pastry flour
1 Tbs. ground coriander
1 Tbs. orange extract

Combine all ingredients and beat 50 strokes. Fill LECITHIN-OILED muffin tins with ⅓ c. of batter. Let rise in warm place for 10 minutes. Bake at 350° for 30-40 minutes.

YIELD: 14 - ⅓ c. muffins

SOY RAISIN PUFFS

¾ c. dry soy beans (2¼ SOAKED)
1½ c. raisins
4 c. hot tap water
6 c. regular oats

½ c. DATE BUTTER or ⅓ c. honey
2½ tsp. salt
½ c. oil (optional)
2 tsp. vanilla

Soak soy beans overnight (POTPOURRI section). Drain off water. Soak raisins in water for at least 15 minutes. Meanwhile cream together last four ingredients and add rolled oats. Drain water from raisins into measuring cup, adding enough water to equal 4 cups. Place 2 c. of this water in blender with soybeans. Blend until creamy, adding more water as mixture thickens. Continue blending 3 more minutes until foamy.

Pour into oat mixture; adding any remaining water and raisins, and mix together well. Allow to sit for 10 minutes for oats to absorb moisture. Spoon into LECITHIN-OILED muffin tins slightly rounding above top. Muffins do not rise during baking. Bake at 350° for 45-50 minutes until golden brown. Cool 10 minutes. Removed from pans.

YIELD: 12 - ⅔ c. muffins or 18 - ½ c. muffins

Variation: For a lighter muffin, when draining water off raisins, set aside ½ c. Then dissolve 2 Tbs. baking yeast in water and let sit until foamy. Add to oat mixture and blended beans. Immediately scoop into tins and bake. DO NOT let rise.

WHOLESOME BREAKFASTS

FLUFFY SOY-CORN MUFFINS

2 c. **SOAKED SOY BEANS**
2 c. water
2 Tbs. honey
2 Tbs. oil

1 tsp. lecithin
2 tsp. salt
¼ c. quick oats
2 c. unrefined corn meal

Blend all ingredients except cornmeal on high until creamy. Pour into bowl and mix in cornmeal. Heat LECITHIN-OILED muffin tin in oven until hot. Remove from oven and fill with batter. Bake at 375° for 45 minutes. May also be baked in a shallow baking pan and cut in squares.

Delicious served with hot applesauce or DRIED FRUIT BUTTER.

YIELD: 1 dozen muffins

Variation: In place of oats use 2 Tbs. sesame seeds and 2 Tbs. coconut or 4 Tbs. wheat germ.

FRESH FRUIT MUFFINS

1 c. finely chopped dates
2 c. regular oats
1 Tbs. vanilla
½ tsp. salt
¼ c. oil (optional)

1 c. coconut (optional)
3 c. blended fresh fruit of your choice
1 c. whole wheat flour
1 c. OAT FLOUR

Mix all ingredients together well. Fill LECITHIN-OILED muffin tins with ⅓ c. of batter. Bake at 350° for 50 minutes. Cool for 10 minutes before removing.

YIELD: 12 - ⅓ c. muffins

For additional muffin recipes,
see BREAD section

QUINCY MARKET FRUIT COBBLER

Make one recipe of DELICIOUS BISCUIT. Roll out ⅔ of dough on floured surface. Put into 8" x 8" baking dish lining bottom and sides. Trim off excess and prick bottom. Roll out remaining dough ⅜" thick. Cut out 9 biscuits with top of glass. Place on cookie sheet. Set biscuits and cobbler

Continued on next page...

crust aside in warm place to rise for 10 minutes. Bake at 350° for 25 minutes. When crust is cooled, fill with 4 cups cooked fruit filling of your choice. Place biscuits on top of fruit. Best served the next day warmed in 250° oven.

YIELD: 1 – 8″ x 8″ cobbler

APPLE BUCKLE

3 c. **OAT FLOUR**
3 c. **whole wheat flour**
2 tsp. **salt**
1 Tbs. **coriander**
1 tsp. **anise**
2 c. **warm water**
2 Tbs. **honey, #1**

2½ Tbs. **baking yeast**
½ c. **soy oil**
1 Tbs. **vanilla**
1 c. **honey, #2**
1 c. **finely chopped apples**

Combine first five dry ingredients in a bowl and stir together well.

In a small bowl mix together next three ingredients. Set aside for 10-15 minutes to bubble in draft-free area to make sponge.

While sponge is bubbling, beat together next three ingredients in a bowl. Set aside. Then finely chop apples.

When sponge is fully bubbled, add liquid ingredients and apples to dry ingredients. Stir together well. Immediately pour batter into 9″ x 13″ LECITHIN-OILED baking dish and spread evenly. Do not let rise, but bake in preheated 375° oven for 15 minutes. Reduce temperature to 350° and bake 25-30 minutes more. The center will spring back to the touch of your finger when done.

While cake is baking, make ½ recipe of OLD-FASHIONED APPLE PIE filling. Then make one recipe of STREUSEL TOPPING. When cake is done and slightly cooled, spread on apple pie filling and sprinkle with STREUSEL TOPPING. Yummy! Best served the next day.

YIELD: 1 - 9″ x 13″ Apple Buckle

BLUEBERRY BUCKLE

Make one recipe APPLE BUCKLE omitting coriander and anis
substituting fresh or frozen blueberries for chopped apples. Whi
baking, make ½ recipe of BLUEBERRY TOPPING using
amount of cornstarch for a filling. Continue with recipe unt
YIELD: 1 - 9″ x 13″ Blueberry Buckle

WHOLESOME BREAKFASTS

STREUSEL TOPPING

1 c. GRANOLA
1 c. coconut
¼ tsp. salt
1½ tsp. water

1 tsp. vanilla
1½ tsp. coriander
½ tsp. anise

Blend first two ingredients high for 15-20 seconds until finely ground. Pour into bowl and add remaining ingredients. Mix together well with hands. Store in refrigerator in covered container.
YIELD: 1¾ c.

SAVORY BREAKFAST IDEAS

SCRAMBLED TOFU

½ c. finely chopped onions
¼ c. water
2 Tbs. oil (olive is best)
2 c. mashed tofu
4 tsp. COUNTRY-STYLE
SEASONING

½ tsp. onion powder
2 tsp. yeast flakes
¼-½ tsp. garlic powder
¼ tsp. salt
2 Tbs. fresh chopped chives or
1 Tbs. dried chives or
parsley (optional)

Rinse tofu in cold water; drain and mash with potato masher or fork. In a skillet, saute onions in water and oil until soft. Add remaining ingredients and stir together well on medium heat 5-10 minutes. Delicious served with POTATO PANCAKES or LATKES, KETCHUP and OVEN FRIES.
YIELD: 2¼ c.
Variation: Add ¼-½ tsp. thyme.

STERN OMELETTE

SCRAMBLED TOFU adding 1 cup chopped
o chopped onions. When tofu is done, add 1
s and 1 c. PIMENTO CHEESE. Stir together
aking dish. Bake at 350° for 45 minutes.

WHOLESOME BREAKFASTS

BISCUITS 'N GRAVY

Make one recipe DELICIOUS BISCUITS. Serve with COUNTRY STYLE GRAVY or CHIPPED TOFU for a down home favorite.

CHIPPED TOFU

1½ c. ¼" cubed tofu	1 Tbs. onion powder
2 c. water #1	1½ Tbs. soy sauce
2 Tbs. COUNTRY-STYLE SEASONING #1	1 Tbs. COUNTRY-STYLE SEASONING #2
2 c. water #2	2 tsp. cornstarch
½ c. cashew pieces	

Rinse and drain tofu. Cut in ¼" cubes. Make broth by adding COUNTRY-STYLE SEASONING #1 to water #1 in saucepan. Add tofu and boil for 20 minutes. Drain.
Using 1 c. of water #2, blend remaining ingredients on high 2-3 minutes. Pour into saucepan; add remaining cup of water #2 and bring to boil stirring constantly. Cook until thick. Add boiled tofu and stir briefly. Serve over toast, pasta, rice, or DELICIOUS BISCUITS.
YIELD: 3½ c.

SAVORY OATS

3 c. regular oats	1 tsp. basil
3 c. water	1 tsp. oregano
2 Tbs. COUNTRY-STYLE SEASONING	2 Tbs. dried parsley
¼ tsp. garlic powder	1 Tbs. olive oil

Put all ingredients into saucepan and stir together briefly. Bring to a boil. Remove from heat and pour into lightly-oiled 8" x 8" baking dish. Bake at 400° for 30-40 minutes.
YIELD: 8" x 8" baking dish

TOFU CHEESE RAREBIT

1 c. cashew pieces
2½ c. water
2 c. tofu
¼ c. oil (may replace with water)
2½ tsp. salt
1 Tbs. COUNTRY-STYLE SEASONING

1 Tbs. onion powder
¼ tsp. garlic powder
¼ c. yeast flakes
½ c. pimentos
¼ c. lemon juice

Blend 1 c. water with cashews on high speed 1-2 minutes until creamy. Pour into saucepan. Blend rest of ingredients with remaining water until smooth. Pour into saucepan with blended cashews. Bring to boil; reduce heat and simmer until thick, stirring constantly. Serve over toast, pasta or grains.

YIELD: 5½ c.

Variation: For an appetizing touch, place thinly sliced raw onion rings and/or tomato slices on toast before pouring cheese on top.

HEARTY BREAKFAST BEANS

4½ c. COOKED NAVY or GREAT NORTHERN BEANS (1 c. dry = 2¼ c. cooked)
2 c. bean liquid or water
1 c. diced onions
2 Tbs. oil

1 c. cashew pieces
1 c. water
½ tsp. salt
2 tsp. onion powder
½ tsp. garlic powder
¼ c. chopped pimentos

Drain liquid off cooked beans to use in recipe.

Saute onions in oil until clear.

Remove from heat and add pimentos. Blend cashews and water on high speed 1-2 minutes until creamy. Add seasonings while blending.

In lightly oiled baking dish combine cooked beans, bean liquid, onion mixture and cashew mixture. Mix together well. Bake 350° for 30-45 minutes until bubbling. Delicious over SESAME BROILER TOAST.

YIELD: 5½ c.

Note: If using salt free beans use 1½ tsp. salt instead of ½ tsp.

WHOLESOME BREAKFASTS

─────── SESAME BROILER TOAST ───────

Cut bread in half diagonally. Place on cookie sheet and toast under broiler. Remove from broiler, turn over and lightly moisten other side with pastry brush dipped into water. Press moistened side into sesame seeds. Then place bread back on cookie sheet, seed side up. Broil until toasted and seeds are lightly browned.

Note: Do not place bread too close to broiler or crust will burn before bread is sufficiently toasted.

─────── EARLY MORNING POTATO PANCAKES ───────

5 c. raw potatoes, ½" cubes
½-1 c. SOY or NUT MILK (use cashews, omit honey & vanilla)
1½ tsp. onion powder

¼ tsp. garlic powder
1¼ tsp. salt
2-3 Tbs. oil (olive is best)
3-5 Tbs. freshly minced parsley or 1½ Tbs. dried

Steam potatoes in about 2 inches of water until tender. Drain. Add remaining ingredients and mash until smooth. Form into patties ¼" thick. Place on LECITHIN-OILED cookie sheet and bake at 400° for 20-40 minutes turning once. Pancakes are done when browned. Serve with fresh parsley, tomatoes and SCRAMBLED TOFU.

YIELD: 9 - ½ c. patties

─────── TOFU POTATO LATKES ───────

2 c. tofu
¼ c. oil
¼ c. water
8 c. grated raw potatoes, packed into cup
1½ c. grated raw onion
¼ c. dried parsley or ½ c. fresh

2 tsp. salt
¾ tsp. garlic powder
½ c. OAT FLOUR
3 Tbs. onion powder
2 Tbs. COUNTRY-STYLE SEASONING

Rinse, drain, crumble tofu with hands and measure. Blend first three ingredients until smooth and pour into large bowl. Add remaining ingredients and mix well. Drop ½ c. portions onto LECITHIN-OILED cookie sheet and flatten. Bake at 400° for 15 minutes. Turn and bake until browned, about 10-15 minutes more.

Continued on next page...

WHOLESOME BREAKFASTS

...Continued from preceding page

YIELD: 20 - 2" latkes or 6-7 9" x 9" waffles

Variation: For waffles, put 1½ c. of mixture on preheated, LECITHIN-OILED waffle iron and bake 10-15 minutes. Nicely browned when done.

OVEN FRIES

8 c. raw fries (about 5 med. potatoes)	1 tsp. salt	
1-2 Tbs. olive oil	2 tsp. onion powder	
	½ tsp. garlic powder	

Wash and scrub potatoes, leaving on the skins. Slice potatoes lengthwise ¼" thick. Cut slices in half lengthwise. Put in bowl and add remaining ingredients. Mix together well. Spread on LECITHIN-OILED cookie sheet. Bake at 400° for 40 minutes Flip and continue baking for 20 minutes more.

YIELD: 4 c. oven fries

LEFTOVER CEREAL & BREAD SUGGESTIONS

Often you will ask yourself, "What do I do with this leftover cereal and these odds and ends of bread?" In our efforts to tackle this problem we have discovered creative solutions we hope you'll enjoy.

Recipes using leftover bread:
  APPLE BREAD-FEST
  OLD-FASHIONED BREAD PUDDING
  APPLE BROWN BETTY
  LAYERED BREAD PUDDING
  BREAD CRUMB GRANOLA
  BREAD WAFFLES
  CASHEW & FLAXSEED FRENCH TOAST

Recipes for using leftover cereal:
  CREAMY RICE PUDDING
  BREAKFAST BANANA SPLITS
  RICE WAFFLES

WHOLESOME BREAKFASTS

AUF-LAUF

1 c. fresh or canned fruit
1 c. DRIED FRUIT BUTTER
½ c. unsweetened fruit juice
¼ tsp. salt
2 Tbs. tahini, peanut butter or other nut butter

4 c. leftover cooked whole grain cereal
¾ c. chopped nuts

Stir together first five ingredients to make fruit mixture.

Layer in 8" x 8" baking dish:
    2 c. leftover cereal
    1 c. fruit mixture
    2 more c. leftover cereal
    remaining fruit mixture
    nuts

Bake at 350° for 30-45 minutes until hot.
YIELD: 8" x 8" baking dish

CEREAL COOKIES

2 c. leftover cooked whole grain cereal
½ c. whole grain flour
2 Tbs. oil
2 Tbs. honey

¼ tsp. salt
2 tsp. vanilla
½ c. chopped nuts or coconut
½ c. chopped dried fruit

Put all ingredients in bowl and mix together well with hands. Drop by rounded tablespoon on LECITHIN-OILED cookie sheet. Bake at 350° for 30-40 minutes.
YIELD: 12 - 2" cookies

LEFTOVER CEREAL SQUARES

When leftover cereal is still warm or hot, pack into a container to mold. Refrigerate until next day. Remove from mold and slice ¼-½" thick. Cut slices into fingers. Place on cookie sheet and spread with DRIED FRUIT BUTTER, applesauce or nut butter of your choice. May top with chopped nuts. Bake at 350° for 20-30 minutes until hot and browned on the edges.

HEALTHFUL DESSERTS

SUPPER FRUIT SOUP

½ c. minute tapioca
5 c. unsweetened pineapple
juice
½ c. chopped dried apricots or
raisins
3 c. unsweetened orange juice
2 c. diced red apples

1⅓ c. chopped oranges (2)
2½ c. thinly sliced bananas
(4 medium)
1 c. unsweetened pineapple
chunks
1¼ c. strawberries, blueberries
or grapes

Soak tapioca in pineapple juice for 30 minutes. Pour into saucepan and cook over medium heat stirring constantly until tapioca is clear. Add remaining ingredients and serve hot. Or chill and serve cold. Delicious served with OAT CRACKERS or ENGLISH SCONES. A perfect light supper.

YIELD: 12 c.

Variation: May use 4 c. pineapple juice and 4 c. orange juice.

PALM FRUIT DRESSING

1 c. SOY MAYONNAISE (omit
onion and garlic powder)
⅓ c. coconut

½ c. crushed pineapple
1 c. mashed bananas

Stir ingredients together in bowl. May serve on fruit salad or as a dip for fresh fruit platter.

YIELD: 2 c.

CAROB FONDUE

Make one recipe of CAROB PIE using only 2 Tbs. cornstarch. After thickening, pour into fondue pot. Dip pieces of fresh fruit into hot carob. Delicious!

STUFFED DRIED FRUIT

Stuff pitted prunes, dates, apricots or figs with nut butter or nuts. Use your imagination for creating combinations. Makes a delightful and simple dessert.

HEALTHFUL DESSERTS

SALTED ROASTED NUTS

⅓ c. hot water
2 tsp. salt

5 c. mixed nuts of your choice

In small bowl stir together first two ingredients until salt is dissolved. In another bowl, make nut mixture. Pour salt water over nuts and stir until nuts are well coated. Spread onto cookie sheet. Bake at 225° for approximately 1½ hours. Stir several times while roasting. A fitting complement to a fresh fruit platter or bowl.

YIELD: 5 c.

Note: If using peanuts, they should be slightly roasted first.

BANANA DATE PUDDING

2 c. water
¾ c. cashew pieces
1 c. pitted dates
1 tsp. vanilla

⅛ tsp. salt
2 Tbs. cornstarch
1¼ c. thinly sliced bananas
(2 medium)

Blend first six ingredients 1-3 minutes on high speed until creamy. Pour into saucepan and bring to a boil, stirring constantly. Cook until thick. Slightly cool. Add sliced bananas. Chill. May serve hot or cold.

YIELD: 3 c.

TAPIOCA PUDDING

3 c. warm water
1 c. cashew pieces
⅓ c. minute tapioca
1 Tbs. vanilla

½ tsp. salt
⅓ c. honey
2 Tbs. liquid lecithin

Blend 1 c. water and cashew on high 1-2 minutes until creamy. Pour into saucepan and add remaining water and rest of ingredients. Cook on medium-high stirring constantly until thick and tapioca is clear. Chill.

YIELD: 3½ c.

CAROB PUDDING

Make one recipe of CAROB PIE filling using only ¼ c. cornstarch.

HEALTHFUL DESSERTS

BLANC MANGE PUDDING

½ c. cashew pieces
4 c. water
⅓ c. honey
½ c. soy milk powder

¼ tsp. salt
1 Tbs. vanilla
3 Tbs. agar flakes

In saucepan soak agar in 3 c. water for 3 minutes. Boil until dissolved, 3-5 minutes. Blend the remaining cup of water and rest of ingredients on high until creamy, 1-2 minutes. Stop blender and add hot agar mixture and blend briefly. Pour into mold or bowl and chill. Serve plain, with a fruit sauce or fresh fruit.

YIELD: 4 c.

HEAVENLY RICE PUDDING

2 c. COOKED BROWN RICE
½ c. chopped dates
1 c. SOY WHIPPED CREAM or
SWEET CASHEW MILK

½ c. chopped nuts
1 c. crushed pineapple
1 c. fresh or frozen berries
(optional)

Mix ingredients together. Bake at 350° for 30 minutes to serve hot. Chill to serve cold.

YIELD: 3 c.

Note: Do not use walnuts or pecans because they will cause discoloration.

CAROB CHEWIES

2 c. brazil nuts
½ c. tahini
½ c. honey

½ c. carob powder
½ tsp. salt
1 tsp. vanilla

Blend brazil nuts on high until ground, stopping blender once or twice to stir contents. Empty into bowl and add remaining ingredients. Mix together well. Roll into ⅛ c. (2 Tbs.) balls. Refrigerate or freeze.

YIELD: 20 - ⅛ c. (2 Tbs.) balls

HEALTHFUL DESSERTS

BUTTER CRUNCHIES

½ c. peanut butter
2 Tbs. honey
2 c. GRANOLA

pinch of salt
1½ tsp. vanilla

Using your hands, mix all ingredients together well in bowl. Dip hands into water and form into balls. May roll in coconut, finely chopped nuts or carob powder. Freeze.
YIELD: 19 - ⅛ c. balls

FUDGY CAROB CHUNKIES

½ c. carob powder
½ c. water
1 c. peanut butter
½ c. coconut
1 c. DATE BUTTER (1 c.
   dates, ½ c. water)

1 c. coarsely chopped walnuts
1 tsp. vanilla
½ c. raisins (optional)

Combine first two ingredients in small saucepan and cook on medium-high until thick, stirring constantly. Remove from heat and add remaining ingredients. Stir together well. Press evenly into 8" x 8" baking dish. Refrigerate. Cut into 1" x 1" squares. Freeze for a chewier fudge.
YIELD: 8" x 8" baking dish or 36 - 1" x 1" squares

MARZIPAN SQUARES

CRUST:
Make ½ recipe of GRANOLA CRUMB CRUST or use 1 c. CRUNCHY ANISE BAR DOUGH. Press evenly into bottom of 8" x 8" baking dish.

MARZIPAN:
2 c. whole BLANCHED
   ALMONDS
⅓ c. honey

½ tsp. salt
2 Tbs. almond extract
1½ c. water

Blend all ingredients on high until smooth, stopping blender once or twice to stir contents. Pour over unbaked crust and spread evenly. Bake at 325° for 35-40 minutes. Cut into 2" squares. This is a traditional European confection.
YIELD: 16 - 2" squares

HEALTHFUL DESSERTS

POLYNESIAN BARS

1 c. dates, packed into cup
¾ c. sulphured apricots,
    packed into cup
2 c. unsweetened orange juice
1 c. millet flour

1¾ c. quick oats
½ tsp. salt
½ c. coconut
1 c. finely chopped walnuts

Soak dates and apricots in 1½ c. orange juice for 10 minutes, then blend on high until fairly smooth. Make millet flour by blending ¾ c. dry millet on high until flour consistency, stopping blender once to stir well. Measure one level cup and pour into bowl. Add remaining ingredients and rest of orange juice, mixing well with hands. Press half of mixture into bottom of 9" x 13" LECITHIN-OILED baking dish. Spread fruit filling evenly on top. Crumble remaining half of mixture over filling. Press into fruit lightly. Bake at 300° for 45-60 minutes.
YIELD: 9" x 13" baking dish

SESAME BARS

⅔ c. honey
¼ c. peanut butter
1 tsp. vanilla

½ tsp. salt
3 c. sesame seeds
1½ c. coconut

In bowl mix together first four ingredients. Add sesame seeds and coconut. Mix well. Press into 9" x 13" LECITHIN-OILED baking dish with hands dipped in water. Bake at 300° for 30-40 minutes. Cool. Cut into squares.
YIELD: 30 - 1½" x 2½" bars

FIG BARS

Make one recipe of CRUNCHY ANISE BARS omitting anise. Divide dough in half. Roll out half of dough evenly in 9" x 13" LECITHIN-OILED cookie sheet. Spread 2½ c. of FIG BUTTER on top. With a damp cloth, moisten counter and place a large piece of plastic over wet area. Put other half of dough in center of plastic and roll into a rectangle the size of cookie sheet. Place pan beside dough. Picking up two corners of plastic farthest from cookie sheet, flip dough onto pan. Press down onto pan and tuck in edges. Cut into bars. Bake at 350° for 30 minutes. Watch carefully.
YIELD: 24 - 3¼" x 1½" bars

HEALTHFUL DESSERTS

GRANOLA BARS

4½ c. regular oats
½ tsp. salt
2 tsp. vanilla
½ c. oil
½ c. honey

2 Tbs. molasses
½ c. finely chopped walnuts
½ c. finely chopped dried
    fruit or carob chips

Put all ingredients into bowl and mix together well with hands. Place mixture into LECITHIN-OILED 9" x 13" baking dish. Press down evenly and firmly with metal spatula. Bake at 400° for 15 minutes. Reverse dish and bake an additional 5 minutes. Watch carefully. Totally cool before cutting.

YIELD: 30 - 1½" x 2½" bars

Suggested fruit/nut combinations: apple/almond, date/walnut or raisin/hazelnut.

CRUNCHY ANISE BARS

¼ c. oil
1 Tbs. liquid lecithin
½ tsp. salt
1 Tbs. vanilla
⅔ c. honey

1 Tbs. anise (ground)
1 c. OAT FLOUR
1½ c. whole wheat pastry flour
    or whole wheat flour

In bowl beat well first six ingredients. Add flours and continue to stir. When dough becomes stiff, mix with hands. Place dough on cookie sheet. Cover with a piece of plastic and roll out evenly. Cut into bars. Bake at 350° for 30 minutes.

YIELD: Approximately 36 - 1" x ¾" bars

Variation: For lemon bars: omit anise and add 1¼ tsp. lemon extract and 1½ tsp. grated lemon rind. For almond bars: omit anise and add 1¼ tsp. almond extract and ¼ c. finely chopped almonds.

Note: If cookie sheet does not have a non-stick coating, be sure to lightly coat with LECITHIN-OIL mixture.

HEALTHFUL DESSERTS

BANANA DATE COOKIES

1½ c. mashed bananas
   (2 medium-large)
1 c. chopped dates
2 c. regular oats or 1 c.
   regular and 1 c. quick
½ c. chopped almonds or
   filberts

¼ c. oil
½ c. DATE BUTTER (optional)
1 tsp. vanilla
½ tsp. salt

Mix ingredients together well in bowl and let sit for 5 minutes. Drop onto lightly-oiled cookie sheet by ⅛ c. (2 Tbs.) portions. Flatten slightly. Bake at 350° for 25 minutes.
YIELD: 23 - ⅛ c. (2 Tbs.) cookies

CAROB COCONUT COOKIES

⅔ c. honey
⅓ c. SOY MILK or water
½ c. oil
1 tsp. vanilla
½ tsp. salt

¼ c. carob powder
1½ c. regular oats
½ c. whole wheat flour
½ c. OAT FLOUR
1 c. coconut

In bowl, stir together well first five ingredients. Mix remaining dry ingredients in another bowl. Add liquids to dry and stir together well. Drop onto LECITHIN-OILED cookie sheet by ⅛ c. (2 Tbs.) portions and flatten. Bake at 350° for 20-22 minutes. Watch carefully.
YIELD: 18 - ⅛ c. (2 Tbs.) cookies

PEANUT BUTTER COOKIES

¾-1 c. honey
2 tsp. vanilla
¾ tsp. salt
½ tsp. lemon extract (optional)

1½ c. peanut butter
¼ c. oil
1 c. whole wheat flour
1 c. OAT FLOUR

In bowl mix all ingredients together well. Form into ⅛ c. (2 Tbs.) balls and place on cookie sheet. Flatten with fork. Bake at 350° for 12-15 minutes. Watch carefully.
YIELD: 27 - ⅛ c. (2 Tbs.) cookies
Variations: May add ½ - 1 c. carob chips.

HEALTHFUL DESSERTS

TAHINI-GRANOLA COOKIES

6 Tbs. tahini	1½ tsp. vanilla
½ tsp. salt	1½ c. regular oats
⅔ c. honey	½ c. GRANOLA of your choice

In bowl mix ingredients together well. Let sit 10 minutes. Drop by ⅛ c. (2 Tbs.) portions onto cookie sheet. Flatten slightly. Bake at 350° for 15-20 minutes or until golden. Remove from oven and let sit for 15 minutes before removing from cookie sheet.

YIELD: 17 - ⅛ c. (2 Tbs.) cookies

HAYSTACK COOKIES

½ c. whole wheat flour	½ c. quick or regular oats
¼ c. honey	2 c. chopped walnuts
2⅓ c. coconut	2 c. DATE BUTTER
1½ tsp. salt	1½ tsp. vanilla

Mix all ingredients together in bowl. Drop by ¼ c. portions onto LECITHIN-OILED cookie sheet. Form into haystack shape with hands. Bake at 350° for 30-40 minutes or until lightly browned.

YIELD: 20 - ¼ c. cookies

CAROB CHIP COOKIES

¾ c. honey	¾ c. chopped walnuts
½ c. oil	1 c. carob chips
1 Tbs. vanilla	2 c. regular oats
1 tsp. salt	2 c. OAT FLOUR or
½ c. SOY MILK	whole wheat flour

In one bowl beat together the first five ingredients. Mix remaining dry ingredients in another bowl. Combine liquid and dry and stir together well. Let sit for 15 minutes. Drop ⅛ c. (2 Tbs.) portions onto LECITHIN-OILED cookie sheet. Flatten slightly and shape. Bake at 350° for 20-25 minutes.

YIELD: 38 - ⅛ c. (2 Tbs.) cookies

HEALTHFUL DESSERTS

OATMEAL RAISIN COOKIES

Make CAROB CHIP COOKIES recipe substituting raisins for carob chips. Plump raisins first by soaking in hot water for 10 minutes. Drain and add to batter. May add ¾ tsp. lemon extract or 1 tsp. grated lemon rind.

LEMON HAZELNUT COOKIES

1¼ c. honey	2 Tbs. lemon extract
1 c. oil	2 Tbs. grated lemon rind
1½ tsp. salt	4 c. OAT FLOUR
¾ c. SOY MILK	1½ c. chopped hazelnuts

In bowl beat together first six ingredients. Add remaining ingredients mixing well. Let sit 15 minutes. Drop ⅛ c. (2 Tbs.) portions onto LECITHIN-OILED cookie sheet. Bake at 350° for 20 minutes. Watch carefully.
YIELD: 43 - ⅛ c. (2 Tbs.) cookies

FUDGY CAROB COOKIES

1 c. honey	¾ c. SOY MILK
2 Tbs. molasses	½ c. carob powder
1 c. oil	1 tsp. coffee substitute
2 Tbs. vanilla	4 c. OAT FLOUR
1½ tsp. salt	1½ c. chopped walnuts

In bowl beat together first six ingredients. Add remaining ingredients and mix together well. Let sit for 10 minutes. Drop by ⅛ c. (2 Tbs.) portions onto LECITHIN-OILED cookie sheet. Bake at 350° for 25 minutes.
YIELD: 40 - ⅛ c. (2 Tbs.) cookies

HEALTHFUL DESSERTS

——— PINWHEEL REFRIGERATOR COOKIES ———

Dark Dough:

¼ c. oil	⅔ c. honey
1 Tbs. liquid lecithin	¾ c. carob powder
1 Tbs. vanilla	1¼ c. whole wheat flour
½ tsp. salt	½ c. OAT FLOUR

In bowl cream together first five ingredients well. Add remaining ingredients. Stir together and then mix well with hands.

Light Dough:

¼ c. oil	⅔ c. honey
1 Tbs. liquid lecithin	1½ c. whole wheat flour
1 Tbs. vanilla	1 c. OAT FLOUR
½ tsp. salt	

In another bowl, make light dough repeating same procedure as above.

To make pinwheels: Moisten surface with damp cloth. Cover with two pieces of plastic wrap set side by side. Place dark dough in center of one piece and roll into rectangle. Place light dough in center of other piece and roll out to same size and shape. Flip light dough on top of dark and remove plastic. Roll together to make a log. Wrap in plastic. Set on cookie sheet and refrigerate for 4-6 hours. Carefully slice ⅜" thick with serrated knife. Put on cookie sheet and bake at 300° for 20-25 minutes. Cool before removing.

YIELD: 31 cookies

——— CARROT MACAROONS ———

1 c. grated raw carrots, packed into cup (about 2 medium-large carrots)	2 Tbs. oil
	1 tsp. almond extract or vanilla
	2 c. coconut
¼ c. water or enough to pour over carrots to fill cup	½ c. whole wheat or OAT FLOUR
½ c. honey	½ tsp. salt

Wash and grate carrots. Pack and measure. Put in bowl. Add remaining ingredients and stir together well. Let sit for 10 minutes. Drop onto LECITHIN-OILED cookie sheet. Shape and flatten slightly. Bake at 350° for 20-25 minutes until nicely browned.

YIELD: 20 - ⅛ c. (2 Tbs.) cookies

HEALTHFUL DESSERTS

FLAKY WHEAT-OAT PIE CRUST

⅓ c. oil
½ c. warm water
1 Tbs. liquid lecithin

1 c. whole wheat flour
1 c. OAT FLOUR
1 tsp. salt

In bowl beat well first three ingredients with a fork. In another bowl stir together flours and salt. Add liquid ingredients to dry, stirring just enough until dough is formed. Do not overmix because crust will be tough. Then press dough together with hands to form ball.

Procedure for rolling out pie crust: With a damp cloth, moisten an area about 12" x 14". Place plastic wrap over wet area. Put half the dough in center of plastic. Then place another piece of plastic over dough. Roll out a 10-11" circle. Remove top plastic. Place inverted pie pan in center of dough. Put one hand on pie pan while using either hand underneath bottom plastic pressing hand into center of pie pan. Flip pie pan over. Press dough carefully into bottom of pie pan. Remove bottom piece of plastic. For prebaked pie shell, prick bottom with fork before baking.

For top crust, roll out between plastic, following preceding steps. Remove top piece. Pick up bottom plastic and flip crust onto pie. Remove bottom piece. Roll edges together and flute.

YIELD: 1 double 9" pie crust

Note: For prebaked pie shell bake at 350° for 20-25 minutes or until fluted edge is firm to the touch.

GRANOLA CRUMB CRUST

3 c. ground GRANOLA
2 tsp. coriander
2-3 Tbs. oil

3-4 Tbs. water
2 Tbs. honey

Blend 2 c. granola on high until fine. Pour into bowl and repeat. (2 c. granola = 1½-1⅔ c. ground). Measure 3 c. ground granola and put in bowl. Add remaining ingredients. Stir together with fork and then mix together well with hands. Add honey only if granola is unsweetened. For baked pie shell, press into bottom and sides of pie pan. Bake at 350° for 30 minutes.

YIELD: 1-9" pie shell or bottom crust for 9" x 13" baking dish

HEALTHFUL DESSERTS

COCONUT-OAT PIE CRUST

1 c. regular oats	¼ tsp. salt
1 c. coconut	4-5 Tbs. water

Blend first two ingredients on high 15-20 seconds until ground. Pour into bowl and add remaining ingredients. Mix together well with hands. Press evenly into 9" pie pan and bake at 400° for 20 minutes.

YIELD: 1-9" pie crust

OLD-FASHIONED APPLE PIE

9 c. sliced unpeeled apples	3 Tbs. cornstarch or OAT FLOUR
1⅛ c. apple juice concentrate	¼ tsp. salt
3 Tbs. water	¾ tsp. coriander

Prepare FLAKY WHEAT-OAT PIE CRUST. Wash, core and slice apples. Put first two ingredients in saucepan and cook on medium for 10 minutes until apples are soft. Stir occasionally. Mix remaining ingredients in small bowl, stir into apples. Cook two minutes more. Spoon into unbaked pie shell. Cover with top crust or lattice. Bake at 350° for 45-60 minutes. Pie crust is done when fluted edge is firm but not hard. For attractive, shiny glaze, brush orange juice concentrate over crust after removing pie from oven. Serve hot or cold.

YIELD: 1 rounded 9" pie

Variation: May sprinkle chopped nuts over apples before putting on top crust.

LEMON PIE

2 c. unsweetened pineapple juice	⅓-½ c. honey
1 c. orange juice	½ tsp. salt
6½ Tbs. cornstarch	¼ c. lemon juice
	1 Tbs. grated lemon rind

Blend all ingredients, except lemon rind, for 20 seconds. Empty into saucepan, add lemon rind and cook on medium-high. Stirring constantly until thick. Pour into a baked pie shell. Chill. May top with SOY WHIPPED CREAM and finely chopped TOASTED NUTS.

YIELD: 1 - 9" pie

HEALTHFUL DESSERTS

FRESH STRAWBERRY PIE

4 c. fresh strawberries, cut
   in quarters lengthwise
¾ c. chopped fresh
   strawberries

1⅓ c. apple juice concentrate
1 tsp. vanilla
pinch of salt
6 Tbs. cornstarch

Wash and stem 3 pints of strawberries. Cut 4 c. of berries lengthwise into quarters and set aside. Chop another ¾ c. of berries and put into blender. Add remaining ingredients and blend on high for 15-20 seconds. Pour into saucepan. Cook on medium-high, stirring constantly until thick. Remove from heat and gently fold in berries with a rubber spatula. Place in baked pie shell and shape. Chill. May top with SOY WHIPPED CREAM or additional fresh strawberries prepared in the following manner: Cut berries lengthwise in ⅛" slices. Place slices side by side covering top of pie with concentrated circles. Put a whole strawberry in the center. Glaze with BERRY SHINY GLAZE.

YIELD: 1 - 9" pie

FRESH BLUEBERRY PIE

5 c. fresh blueberries
1 c. apple juice concentrate
½ c. RUNNY DATE BUTTER

pinch of salt
1 tsp. vanilla
¼ c. cornstarch

Wash 5 c. of berries. Put 4 c. of berries aside. Blend remaining cup with rest of ingredients on high for 20 seconds. Pour into saucepan and cook on medium-high stirring constantly until thick. Remove from heat and gently fold in berries with rubber spatula. Put into baked pie shell and shape. Chill. May top with SOY WHIPPED CREAM.

YIELD: 1 - 9" pie

BLUEBERRY PIE SURPRISE
(subtley semi-sweet)

5 c. frozen blueberries
¾ c. apple juice concentrate
¼ tsp. salt

6½ Tbs. cornstarch
7 Tbs. apple juice concentrate

Continued on next page...

Put first three ingredients into saucepan and bring to boil on medium-high stirring often. Boil for three minutes. Berries will emit juice as they cook. While berries are cooking stir together remaining ingredients in small bowl. Add to berries stirring constantly. Reduce heat and continue to cook for one more minute while stirring. Spread evenly into baked pie shell. Chill. Delicious topped with SOY WHIPPED CREAM.

YIELD: 1 - 9" pie

VERY BERRY PIE

1¼ c. pineapple juice or apple juice concentrate
½ c. honey
1 tsp. vanilla

6½ Tbs. cornstarch
4 c. frozen raspberries, blackberries or boysenberries

Blend first four ingredients on high for 10 seconds. Pour into saucepan and cook over medium-high stirring constantly until thick. Remove from heat and gently fold in berries with rubber spatula. Put into baked pie shell and chill.

YIELD: 1 - 9" pie

PINEAPPLE-COCONUT PIE

1⅓ c. unsweetened pineapple juice
⅔ c. unsweetened orange juice
1 tsp. vanilla
¼ tsp. salt

6 Tbs. cornstarch
½ c. shredded coconut
2 c. crushed pineapple sliced bananas

Briefly blend first five ingredients on high. Pour into saucepan and cook on medium-high heat until clear stirring constantly. Remove from heat and stir in coconut and pineapple. Line baked pie shell with sliced bananas and cover with filling. Chill. May sprinkle with coconut before chilling, or chill first and top with SOY WHIPPED CREAM and chopped nuts before serving.

YIELD: 1 - 9" pie

HEALTHFUL DESSERTS

CAROB PIE

4 c. **BASIC NUT MILK (use cashew pieces, omit honey, vanilla and salt)**
½ c. **honey or 1¼ c. DATE BUTTER**
¼ c. **coconut (optional)**

6 Tbs. **cornstarch or ¼ c. cornstarch and ¼ c. whole wheat flour**
1 tsp. **coffee substitute**
4-6 Tbs. **carob powder**
½ tsp. **salt**
1 tsp. **vanilla**

Blend all ingredients on high until creamy. Empty into a saucepan and cook over medium-high stirring constantly until thick. Pour into baked pie shell. May sprinkle with coconut. Cover top with plastic to prevent a hard film from forming. Chill. After chilling, may top with SOY WHIPPED CREAM and then TOASTED COCONUT or coconut dusted in carob powder.
YIELD: 1 - 10" pie

CAROB-MINT PIE

Make one recipe of CAROB PIE adding 1 tsp. peppermint flavoring.

COCONUT CREAM PIE

1 c. **SOY MILK or water**
⅔ c. **honey**
2 tsp. **coconut flavoring**
½ c. **cashew pieces**
⅓ c. **cornstarch**
1½ tsp. **salt**
1 c. **crumbled tofu**

4 tsp. **vanilla**
1¼ c. **water #1**
½ c. **coconut**
2 Tbs. **agar flakes**
1 c. **water #2**
1-2 c. **coconut**

Blend first eight ingredients on high until creamy. Pour into sauce pan. Add water #1 to sauce pan and cook on medium high until thick, stirring constantly. Set aside. Put next three ingredients into another sauce pan and bring to boil. Reduce heat and simmer 10 minutes then stir into cashew mixture. Lastly fold in the 1-2 c. of coconut. Pour into baked pie shell and chill.
YIELD: 1 - 10" pie
Variation: May use TOASTED COCONUT

HEALTHFUL DESSERTS

MAPLE WALNUT PIE

2½ c. hot water
¼ c. flaxseed
3 Tbs. cornstarch
1 c. pitted dates
½ tsp. salt
1 tsp. vanilla

2 tsp. maple
2 Tbs. oil
⅓ c. honey
1½ c. coarsely chopped
TOASTED WALNUTS

Blend on high: ½ c. water, flaxseed and cornstarch. As mixture begins to thicken, add another cup of water, continuing to blend until it thickens again. Pour into bowl. Blend remaining cup of water and rest of ingredients, except walnuts, on high until smooth. Empty into bowl and add TOASTED WALNUTS. Mix together. Pour into unbaked pie shell. Bake at 350° for 50-60 minutes. Pie will rise during baking and fall as it cools.

YIELD: 1 - 10" pie

Variation: May use pecans.

PUMPKIN PIE

6 Tbs. cashews
¾ c. water
1⅔ c. pumpkin
¼ c. honey
2 Tbs. molasses

½ tsp. salt
2 tsp. coriander
1½ tsp. vanilla
2 Tbs. cornstarch

Blend first two ingredients on high until creamy, 1-2 minutes. Pour into bowl. Add remaining ingredients and mix together well. Put into pie shell and bake at 350° for one hour or until pie is just about set in center.

YIELD: 1 - 9" pie

Note: If using fresh pumpkin or squash, wash and remo~ seeds. Cut into chunks, steam and puree. Leaving the skin on is th ~~et to a rich pumpkin color.

BUTTERSCOTCH

¾ c. coarsely grated carrots
1 c. water
3 c. SOY MILK
¾ c. dates, packed into cup
¾ tsp. salt

2 tsp
2 ts
1/
2

Cook carrots in water until tender. Place in blender and add remaining ingredients. Blend on high until creamy. Pour into saucepan and cook over medium-high stirring constantly until thick. Fill pre-baked pie shell and chill. Serve with SOY WHIPPED CREAM.

YIELD: 1 - 9″ pie

Variation: For pudding, use ¼ c. cornstarch.

SOY WHIPPED CREAM #1

¾ c. **SOY MILK**
2 Tbs. **honey**
¼-½ tsp. **vanilla**

pinch of **salt**
¾ c. **soy, corn or safflower oil**
⅛-¼ tsp. **lemon juice**

Blend first four ingredients on high for 5-10 seconds. Slowly dribble in oil, blending for an additional full minute after all the oil has been added. Stop blender and fold in lemon juice. Put into covered container and chill.

YIELD: 2 c.

Variations:

1. CAROB CREAM: Add 2-3 Tbs. carob powder to first four ingredients.
2. STRAWBERRY OR BLUEBERRY CREAM: When cream is finished, fold in STRAWBERRY or BLUEBERRY TOPPING until desired color is attained.

Note: May use commercial soy milk, such as Eden Soy.

SOY WHIPPED CREAM #2
(with Soygen)

¾ c. **water**
½ c. **Soyagen**
1 tsp. **vanilla**
⅛ tsp. **salt**

2-3 Tbs. **honey**
¾-1 c. **oil**
¼-½ tsp. **lemon juice**

Blend first five ingredients on high for 10 seconds. Leaving blender running, remove top and very slowly dribble in oil until mixture thickens. Stop blender and fold in lemon juice. Chill.

YIELD: 1⅓ c.

riations:

ROB – add 2 Tbs. carob powder and ¼ tsp. coffee substitute. Use

d 1 Tbs. carob powder, 1 Tbs. coffee substitute and ⅛ tsp.

sp. almond extract; omit vanilla.

HEALTHFUL DESSERTS

SOY WHIPPED CREAM #3
(with SOY BASE)

½ c. water
½ c. SOY BASE
½ tsp. vanilla
¼ tsp. salt

3-4 Tbs. honey
1¼ c. oil
¼-½ tsp. lemon juice

Blend first five ingredients on high for 15-20 seconds. Leaving blender on high, dribble in oil very slowly until unable to blend further. Turn off blender and stir in lemon juice. Chill in covered container.

YIELD: 2 c.

Note: May use same variations as WHIPPED CREAM made with Soyagen.

TOFU WHIPPED CREAM

2 c. tofu
4 tsp. vanilla
½ c. honey

½ tsp. salt
½ c. oil

Rinse tofu and drain. Crumble with hands and measure. Blend all ingredients on high until smooth, stopping blender 2-3 times to stir content. Keep refrigerated.

YIELD: 2¾ c.

TOFU ORANGE WHIPPED CREAM

Make one recipe TOFU WHIPPED CREAM, reducing honey to ¼ c. and add ¼ c. orange juice concentrate.

YIELD: 2 c.

LEMON SAUCE

1 c. cold pineapple juice
pinch of salt
2 Tbs. cornstarch

2½ Tbs. lemon juice
1 tsp. grated lemon rind
1 Tbs. honey

Blend all ingredients briefly on high. Pour into saucepan and cook on medium-high stirring constantly until thick and clear. Delicious over DATE NUT CAKE.

YIELD: 1 c.

HEALTHFUL DESSERTS

BERRY SHINY GLAZE

⅓ c. fresh raspberries or strawberries

⅔ c. apple juice concentrate
4 tsp. cornstarch

Blend all ingredients on high for one minute until creamy. Pour into saucepan and cook over medium-high stirring constantly until thick and clear. Delightful over FRESH STRAWBERRY PIE or CHARLOTTE.
YIELD: ¾ c.

CAROB PEANUT BUTTER ICING

½ c. water
¼-½ c. carob powder
¼ c. water
¾ c. DATE BUTTER

½ c. peanut butter or almond butter
1 tsp. vanilla
¼ tsp. salt

Put first two ingredients in saucepan and cook on medium-high, stirring constantly until thick. Remove from heat. Add remaining ingredients and mix together well.
YIELD: 1¾ c.

COCONUT WALNUT ICING

¾ c. SOY MILK
½ tsp. maple flavoring
1 tsp. vanilla
¼ c. soy margarine
1 Tbs. cornstarch

⅓ c. honey
1 c. coconut
1 c. finely chopped walnuts or pecans

Put first six ingredients in saucepan and cook over medium-high stirring constantly until thick. Remove from heat. Add coconut and nuts. Stir together well. Chill.
YIELD: 2 c.

HEALTHFUL DESSERTS

FUDGY CAROB BROWNIES

1 c. whole wheat flour
1 c. OAT FLOUR
1 c. coarsely chopped walnuts
½ c. oil
1 c. honey
4 tsp. vanilla

2 tsp. liquid lecithin (optional)
⅔ c. SOY or NUT MILK
(using cashews)
1 tsp. salt
1½ tsp. coffee substitute
½ c. carob powder

Before making brownies, preheat oven to 375° and LECITHIN-OIL an 8" x 8" baking dish. In bowl stir together first three ingredients. Blend remaining ingredients on high for one minute. Pour into dry ingredients and fold together quickly. Spread batter into baking dish and bake at 375° for 15 minutes. Reduce heat to 350° and bake 15 minutes more. Do not over bake. Cool. Cut into squares. May frost with CAROB PEANUT BUTTER ICING or CAROB "HOT FUDGE" TOPPING.

YIELD: 16 - 2" x 2" brownies

BANANA DATE NUT CAKE

½ c. warm water
1 Tbs. honey
2 Tbs. active dry yeast
⅓ c. honey
1 Tbs. vanilla
½ c. oil
2 c. mashed ripe bananas (4)

1½ c. whole wheat flour
1½ c. OAT FLOUR or whole
wheat pastry flour
2 tsp. salt
1 c. chopped nuts
2 c. chopped dates

In small bowl, stir together first three ingredients to make sponge. Set aside to bubble in warm place. In another bowl, add next three liquids and bananas, mixing well. In last bowl, stir together remaining ingredients. When sponge is formed, pour contents of first two bowls into last bowl. Mix well briefly. Spread evenly into LECITHIN-OILED 8" x 12" baking dish. Cover and let rise in warm place 10-15 minutes. Bake at 375° for 10 minutes. Reduce heat to 350° and bake 35-40 minutes more. May frost if desired.

YIELD: 8" x 12" cake

HEALTHFUL DESSERTS

DATE-NUT CAKE

⅓-½ c. orange juice
⅓ c. DATE BUTTER
1 tsp. vanilla
2 Tbs. vegetable oil

½ tsp. salt
1 c. whole wheat flour
2 c. chopped dates
2 c. coarsely chopped walnuts

Mix ingredients together in bowl. Spoon into LECITHIN-OILED loaf or bundt pan. Bake at 300° for 50-60 minutes. Cool before removing from pan. Delicious topped with lemon sauce.

YIELD: 1 medium loaf pan (8½" x 4½" x 2½")

FESTIVE FRUIT CAKE

1 can (20 oz.) unsweetened
pineapple chunks
1 tsp. salt
1 c. dates
1 c. dried pears
1 c. dried apricots
1 c. raisins
1 Tbs. grated lemon rind
1 Tbs. grated orange rind

2 tsp. coriander
½ tsp. anise
1 tsp. vanilla
3 Tbs. orange juice concentrate
¾ c. pineapple juice
3 c. walnuts or pecans
1½ c. whole wheat flour
¼ tsp. almond extract
2 Tbs. oil

Dissolve salt in pineapple juice. Cut dates, pears and apricots into approximately ½" pieces. Mix all ingredients together well in bowl. Pack into LECITHIN-OILED bread pan using either one large (9¼"x5¼" x 2¾") or two medium (8½" x 4½" x 2½). Bake at 300° for 2 hours using larger pan or 1½ hours using medium pans.

YIELD: 1 large cake or 2 medium cakes

STRAWBERRY SHORTCAKE

Wash and stem fresh strawberries. Slice in half lengthwise. Put in bowl and add 3-4 Tbs. honey for 8 c. of sliced berries. Cover and refrigerate overnight. Next day, serve over DELICIOUS BISCUITS topped with SOY WHIPPED CREAM. Scrumptious.

Variation: May use frozen strawberries. Leaving whole, marinate in honey overnight at room temperature.

HEALTHFUL DESSERTS

—— SIMPLE CHARLOTTE ——

(A French dessert of bread layered with fruit,
whipped cream, jam or custard)

1½-1¾ lb.	loaf of unsliced whole grain bread	2 c.	water
1 recipe	SOY WHIPPED CREAM	½ c.	cashew pieces
¼ c.	finely chopped nuts	1 tsp.	vanilla
1½ pints	fresh strawberries	⅛ tsp.	salt
		3 Tbs.	honey

Cut off bottom crust of bread. Then cut loaf lengthwise into four ½" slices (3" x 7"). Remove remaining crusts. Place slices on cookie sheet and ZWIEBACK for 30 minutes at 250°. While bread is drying, make one recipe SOY WHIPPED CREAM. Finely chopped nuts of your choice. Rinse and stem strawberries. Finely chop 1 c. berries. Blend last five ingredients on high 1-2 minutes until creamy. Pour cashew milk into 8" x 8" baking dish.

To assemble Charlotte:

Soak 2 slices of zwiebacked bread in cashew milk for 5-7 minutes, flipping 2-3 times. Bread should be softened throughout but not soggy. Repeat with remaining slices. Place one slice of bread on plate. Cover with 2 Tbs. WHIPPED CREAM. Sprinkle with 1 Tbs. nuts. Top with ⅓ c. strawberries. Repeat procedure two more times and top with fourth slice of bread. Frost entire cake with ⅔ c. WHIPPED CREAM. Cut 6 whole strawberries in half lengthwise. Place halves on top of cake. Drizzle on BERRY SHINY GLAZE. Chill overnight.

YIELD: 1 - 3" x 7" x 3" Charlotte

Variations:

1. May use jam between layers.
2. May use fresh raspberries. Will need 2 pints. Forty berries garnish top of cake.
3. May replace SOY WHIPPED CREAM with MOCHA CAROB or ALMOND WHIPPED CREAM.
4. May replace cashews in milk with TOASTED HAZELNUTS, TOASTED WALNUTS, or almonds.

—— WAFFLE CAKE ——

Make one recipe BEST CORN-OAT WAFFLES. When waffles are cooled, invert plate on one waffle cutting around edge to make circle. Repeat for each waffle.

Continued on next page...

HEALTHFUL DESSERTS

To make cake: Place one waffle on plate. Frost with CAROB "HOT FUDGE" TOPPING or CAROB PEANUT BUTTER ICING. Place another waffle over carob. Lightly frost with SOY WHIPPED CREAM followed by a layer of fresh sliced strawberries. Repeat until cake is completed. Ice with CAROB "HOT FUDGE" TOPPING and/or SOY WHIPPED CREAM. Sprinkle with finely chopped TOASTED NUTS. Chill. A real people-pleaser.

Variations: Use your imagination to invent other layering combintions such as sliced bananas and SUMMER FRUIT CREAM; fresh raspberries and MOCHA WHIPPED CREAM, etc.

TOFU CHEESECAKE

Crust:
Make one recipe GRANOLA CRUMB CRUST and press evenly into bottom of 9" x 13" baking dish.

Filling:

4 c. mashed tofu	¼ c. pineapple juice
2 Tbs. vanilla	½ tsp. lemon extract or 1 Tbs.
1½ tsp. salt	lemon juice
⅔ c. honey	½ tsp. coriander
½ c. oil	

Rinse, drain, mash and measure tofu. Put tofu in bowl and add remaining ingredients. Stir together well. Blend half of filling on high until velvety smooth, stopping blender 2-3 times to stir contents. Pour over crust. Repeat procedure with other half. Spread filling evenly over crust. Bake at 350° for 20-30 minutes until edges are lightly browned and middle is firm.

Remove from oven. Cool slightly. Cover with 4 c. STRAWBERRY or BLUEBERRY TOPPING.

YIELD: 1 - 9" x 13" cheesecake

HEALTHFUL DESSERTS

CAROB TOFU CHEESECAKE

3 c. crumbled tofu	¼ c. carob powder
1 c. DATE BUTTER	¼ c. oil
½ tsp. coffee substitute	⅓ c. honey
¾ tsp. salt	½ c. SOY MILK
2 tsp. vanilla	

Make two thirds of a recipe of the GRANOLA CRUMB CRUST and press evenly into bottom of 8 x 8 baking dish. Rinse and crumble tofu. Measure and put in bowl. Add remaining ingredients and stir together well. Blend half of mixture on high until creamy, stopping blender once or twice to stir contents. Pour over crust. Repeat procedure with remaining half. Bake at 350° for 25-30 minutes. Chill. Serve topped with STRAWBERRY TOPPING or fresh sliced strawberries and SOY WHIPPED CREAM.

YIELD: 8" x 8" baking dish or 1 - 9" pie

CARROT CAKE

½ c. warm water	¼ c. coconut
2 Tbs. dry yeast	2-2½ c. whole wheat flour or
2 tsp. honey	whole wheat pastry flour
1½ c. finely grated carrots	½ c. SOY MILK
½ c. chopped walnuts	½ c. oil
1½ tsp. grated orange or lemon	¾ c. honey
rind	¾ tsp. salt
1½ tsp. coriander	1 tsp. vanilla
pinch of anise (optional)	1 tsp. maple flavoring

Combine first three ingredients in small bowl. Set aside in warm place to bubble for about 10 minutes. While sponge is forming; wash, grate and measure carrots. Put into another bowl and add next six ingredients. Mix together well. Blend remaining ingredients on high for one minute. Add to carrots and mix together. When sponge is ready, add to bowl and stir together quickly. Evenly spread into LECITHIN-OILED 8" x 8" baking dish. Bake at 375° for 15 minutes. Reduce heat to 350° and continue baking for 40-45 minutes more. Cake is done when toothpick inserted in center comes out clean.

YIELD: 1 - 8" x 8" cake

Variation: May make into muffins. Ice with SOY WHIPPED CREAM and dip into coconut.

HEALTHFUL DESSERTS

PEACH ICE CREAM

1 c. cashew pieces
1 tsp. vanilla
¼-⅓ c. honey

2½ c. peach liquid and water
3 Tbs. orange juice concentrate
2 c. peach halves

Blend all ingredients on high until creamy, 1-2 minutes. May add fresh fruit and then freeze. After freezing, melt slightly, blend again and refreeze. Serve.

YIELD: 4 c.

Note: Blending and refreezing assures a soft texture to ice cream.

BANANA POPS

Peel bananas. Cut in half and put on popsicle sticks or forks. Ice with DATE BUTTER, CAROB PEANUT BUTTER ICING, CAROB "HOT FUDGE" TOPPING, or nut butter of your choice. Roll in finely chopped nuts, coconut or sunflower seeds. Place bananas on plate and freeze.

MEATLESS ENTREES

HARVEST NUT ROAST

1½ c. chopped onions
3 Tbs. water
2 Tbs. oil (olive is best)
2½ c. finely chopped celery
¾ c. chopped walnuts
¾ c. ground pecans or
sunflower seeds

1½ tsp. salt
2 c. SOY MILK
1¼ tsp. basil
½ tsp. sage or 1¼ tsp. thyme
3 c. whole grain BREAD
CRUMBS

Saute onions in water and oil until clear. Put into bowl and add remaining ingredients, omitting bread crumbs. Stir together well. Fold in bread crumbs. Pour into LECITHIN-OILED 8" x 8" baking dish. Bake at 350° for 60 minutes. To prevent overbrowning on top, may need to cover with foil near end of baking. Delicious served with COUNTRY STYLE GRAVY.
YIELD: 6 c. or 8" x 8" baking dish or medium loaf pan

COUNTRY STYLE GRAVY

2 c. water
½ c. cashew pieces or 3 Tbs.
whole wheat flour
1 Tbs. onion powder
¼ tsp. garlic powder

¼ tsp. salt
2 Tbs. oil (omit if using nuts)
3 Tbs. soy sauce or GOMASIO
1 Tbs. yeast flakes
1 Tbs. cornstarch

Blend all ingredients on high 2-3 minutes until creamy. Pour into saucepan and cook on medium-high until thick, stirring constantly. Serve over entree roasts or loaves, potatoes, or biscuits.
YIELD: 2½ c.

MEATLESS ENTREES

BREAD DRESSING ROAST

6 c.	whole grain bread cubes, ½" x ½"	2½ Tbs.	COUNTRY-STYLE SEASONING
½ tsp.	marjoram	¼ tsp.	salt
¼ tsp.	thyme	¼ tsp.	garlic powder
¼ tsp.	rosemary	1½ tsp.	dried parsley
¼ tsp.	savory	½ c.	canned, drained water chestnuts or chopped TOASTED ALMONDS (optional)
pinch	of sage		
3-4 Tbs.	olive oil		
1½ c.	chopped onions		
1 c.	chopped celery		
3 c.	water		

Place bread cubes on cookie sheet and toast in 350° oven for 20 minutes. In skillet, saute next five ingredients in olive oil for one minute on medium-high stirring constantly. Add onions and celery and stir together well, continuing to cook for 5 more minutes. Put into bowl. In saucepan, bring to boil and stir next five ingredients. Add to bowl along with toasted bread cubes and last ingredient. Mix together well. Put into LECITHIN-OILED 8" x 8" baking dish. Cover and bake at 400° for 25 minutes. Uncover and bake 5 minutes. A holiday favorite served with baked potatoes and COUNTRY STYLE GRAVY.

YIELD: 8 c.

SQUASH NESTS

3 medium acorn squash
1 recipe HARVEST NUT ROAST or BREAD DRESSING

Wash and cut squash in half lengthwise. Remove seeds, pulp and stem. Put ½" water in 2 - 9" x 13" baking dishes. Place squash in water face up. Bake at 350° for 30 minutes or until half cooked. Remove from oven and fill center, slightly mounding, with HARVEST NUT ROAST or BREAD DRESSING. Return to oven and bake at 350° for 1¼ hours.

YIELD: 6 squash nests

MEATLESS ENTREES

BRITISH LENTIL LOAF

1¾ c. dry lentils (about 4 c. cooked)
2¼ c. chopped onions
1 tsp. minced garlic
2 Tbs. oil (olive is best)
1½ c. tomato puree
½ c. SOY MILK

1½ c. chopped celery
3 Tbs. chopped green pepper
¾ tsp. sage
2 tsp. salt
1 Tbs. onion powder
1 c. chopped walnuts
¼ c. whole wheat flour

Put lentils into pot. Cover with water three inches above lentils. Bring to boil. Reduce heat, cover and simmer until tender. Drain and put into bowl. Saute onions and garlic in oil. Add to lentils along with remaining ingredients. Stir together well. Put into LECITHIN-OILED 8″x8″ baking dish. Bake at 350° for 1 hour. Remove from oven. Cover with 1 c. KETCHUP and bake for 15 more minutes.

YIELD: 8 c. or 8″x8″ baking dish

CASHEW LOAF

1 c. chopped onions
2 Tbs. oil (olive is best)
3 Tbs. water
2 c. COOKED BROWN RICE
¾ c. finely chopped celery
1 c. cashew pieces
1½ c. SOY MILK
2 Tbs. soy sauce or GOMASIO
1 tsp. salt

4 Tbs. minced fresh parsley or 2 Tbs. dried
1 Tbs. yeast flakes (optional)
1 Tbs. onion powder
½ tsp. thyme
½ tsp. ground celery seed
½ tsp. sage (optional)
2 c. whole grain BREAD CRUMBS

Saute onions in water and oil. Put into bowl and add remaining ingredients, fold in bread crumbs last. Pour into LECITHIN-OILED 8″x8″ baking dish. Bake at 350° for 1 hour.

YIELD: 6 c. or 8″x8″ baking dish.

MEATLESS ENTREES

MILLET LOAF

2 minced garlic cloves	1 tsp. basil
3-4 Tbs. olive oil	1 tsp. salt
1 c. uncooked millet	2 tsp. onion powder
2 c. chopped onions	½ tsp. oregano
1½ c. chopped celery	2 tsp. honey
6 c. canned tomatoes	½ c. chopped black olives
measured without juice	½ c. cashew pieces (optional)

In pot saute garlic in olive oil. Add next three ingredients and continue to saute for 20 more minutes. Briefly blend on high 3 c. of canned tomatoes. Add to millet. Repeat procedure with rest of tomatoes. Add remaining ingredients except cashews. Stir together well. Bring to boil. Reduce heat, cover and simmer until liquid is absorbed (about 45-60 minutes). Remove from heat. Stir in cashews. Put into LECITHIN-OILED 8" x 8" baking dish. Bake at 350° for 30 minutes.

YIELD: 8 c. or 8" x 8" baking dish

PEANUT BUTTER-CARROT LOAF

⅔ c. peanut butter	1½ tsp. basil
1 c. tomato puree	3 c. shredded carrots
1 Tbs. onion powder	¾ c. water
1¾ tsp. salt	4½ c. whole grain BREAD
1 tsp. garlic powder	CRUMBS

In bowl, cream first six ingredients together with fork. Add remaining ingredients and stir together well. Put into LECITHIN-OILED 8" x 8" baking dish. Cover with foil and bake at 350° for 30-40 minutes. Uncover and bake until browned, about 15 more minutes.

YIELD: 6 c. or 8" x 8" baking dish

Note: Try the following delightful and attractive way to serve this entree. Bake in a bundt pan. Invert onto platter covered with lettuce and fill the center with fresh steamed peas. May place black olives around outside edge of platter.

MEATLESS ENTREES

PECAN LOAF

4 c. ground pecans
2 c. chopped onions
¼ c. water
1 Tbs. salt
1 Tbs. onion powder

1 tsp. garlic powder
4½ c. tomato juice
8 c. whole grain BREAD CRUMBS
2 c. KETCHUP

Grind pecans 2 c. at a time in blender or food processor until meal. Measure and put into bowl. In skillet saute onions in water and add to bowl along with remaining ingredients except KETCHUP. Mix together well with spoon and then hands. Spread evenly into LECITHIN-OILED 8" x 8" baking dish. Bake at 350° for 45 minutes. Then cover with KETCHUP and bake an additional 15 more minutes.

YIELD: 8½ c. or 8" x 8" baking dish

Variation: May use walnuts in place of pecans. Reduce tomato juice to 3½ c.

TOFU LOAF

2 c. chopped onions
2 Tbs. oil (olive is best)
2 Tbs. water
3 c. crumbled tofu
3 c. COOKED BROWN RICE
½ c. SOY MILK
½ c. chopped walnuts
½ tsp. salt

½ tsp. garlic powder
1 Tbs. onion powder
2 Tbs. COUNTRY-STYLE SEASONING
1 Tbs. yeast flakes
⅛ scant tsp. cumin
2 Tbs. soy sauce, unfermented

Saute onions in oil and water. Rinse, drain, crumble and measure tofu. Put tofu into bowl. Add onions and remaining ingredients. Stir together well. Put into LECITHIN-OILED 8" x 8" baking dish. Bake at 350° for 30-45 minutes.

YIELD: 6 c. or 8" x 8" baking dish

Variation: May make into croquettes with ice cream scoop.

MEATLESS ENTREES

BASIC LOAF RECIPE
(for the creative cook)

1 c. chopped vegetables:
onions, green peppers,
celery or mushrooms
1-2 minced garlic cloves
(optional)
2 Tbs. oil
3 Tbs. water
2 c. cooked grain or legume
½ c. chopped nuts or whole
seeds

1½ c. liquid SOY or NUT MILK,
tomato juice or broth
Season-
ings to
taste: salt, herbs, onion or garlic
powder
1-1½ c. whole grain BREAD
CRUMBS

Our basic loaf recipe allows you to create your own entree. Use your imagination as you follow the guidelines above. Some of the best entrees have come from the creative cook.

Basic Procedure: Saute vegetables and garlic in oil and water. Put into bowl. Mix together all ingredients. Bake at 350° for 45-60 minutes in a LECITHIN-OILED 8" x 8" pan or loaf pan.

OATBURGER BAKE

8 c. fresh sliced mushrooms
½ c. olive oil
½ c. water
1 tsp. salt

½ tsp. garlic powder
1 tsp. onion powder
1 recipe OATBURGERS
1 recipe COUNTRY STYLE GRAVY

In skillet, cook mushrooms with next five ingredients until soft. Remove from heat. If using frozen or refrigerated OATBURGERS, be sure to warm in oven before assembling entree. Line the bottom of LECITHIN-OILED 9" x 13" baking dish with 1 c. COUNTRY STYLE GRAVY. Then layer with the following:

8 OATBURGERS
Half of sauteed mushrooms
¾ c. gravy
7 burgers
remainder of mushrooms
¾ c. gravy

Bake at 350° for 20 minutes or until hot.
YIELD: 9" x 13" baking dish

MEATLESS ENTREES

BRAZILIAN RICE

2 c. sliced onions
2 c. green pepper strips
2 Tbs. olive oil
3 Tbs. water
2 c. COOKED BROWN RICE
2½ c. canned tomatoes in puree
½ c. chopped black olives
(optional)

½ c. chopped Brazil nuts
(optional)
1 c. PIMENTO CHEESE
SAUCE
¾ tsp. caraway seeds
½ tsp. salt
¾ tsp. paprika

Saute onions and peppers in oil and water until soft. Put into bowl and add remaining ingredients. Stir together well. Pour into LECITHIN-OILED 8" x 8" baking dish. Bake at 350° for 30-40 minutes.
YIELD: 6½ c. or 8" x 8" baking dish

BROCCOLI ALMONDINE

3½ c. COOKED BROWN RICE
4½ c. slightly steamed broccoli
flowers (about 2 lbs. fresh
broccoli)
4 c. QUICK MUSHROOM
SOUP

1 Tbs. onion powder
1 tsp. salt
½ tsp. garlic powder
1-1½ c. SESAME-ALMOND
TOPPING

Cut flowers off broccoli. Steam lightly until crisp and tender. Combine all ingredients except broccoli in bowl and mix together well. Gently fold in broccoli flowers. Put into LECITHIN-OILED 8" x 8" baking dish. Bake at 350° for 45-60 minutes. Remove from oven and cover with SESAME-ALMOND TOPPING.
YIELD: 7 c. or 8" x 8" baking dish

SESAME-ALMOND TOPPING

1⅓ c. sesame seeds (with hull)
2¾ c. slivered or sliced almonds
2 tsp. salt

3 Tbs. lemon juice
2½ Tbs. olive oil

Put all ingredients into bowl and stir together well. Spread evenly on cookie sheet and bake at 350° for 15-20 minutes until lightly browned.
YIELD: 4 c.
Note: May slice almonds in food processor. If unavailable, chop by hand.

MEATLESS ENTREES

KASHA AU GRATIN

1¼ c. water
½ tsp. salt
⅔ c. buckwheat groats
1¼ c. chopped onions
1 Tbs. olive oil
1 c. partially steamed fresh
   cauliflower (may use
   frozen)

2 c. PIMENTO CHEESE
   SAUCE
1½ tsp. onion powder
½ tsp. garlic powder
½ tsp. salt

Place first two ingredients in saucepan and bring to boil. Stir several times to distribute salt. Add buckwheat and reduce heat. Cover and simmer 20 minutes until water is absorbed. Remove from heat. In skillet, saute onions in olive oil. In saucepan partially steam fresh cauliflower in an inch of water. When using frozen, place in colander and run under hot water for 10-15 seconds and drain. In bowl, combine cooked buckwheat, sauteed onions, cauliflower and remaining ingredients. Stir together well. Put in LECITHIN-OILED 8" x 8" baking dish. Bake at 350° for 35 minutes.
YIELD: 5 c. or 8" x 8" baking dish

MACARONI AU GRATIN

1 minced garlic clove
1 Tbs. olive oil
1 c. chopped onions
1 c. frozen green peas or
   chopped asparagus
1 tsp. salt

4 c. cooked whole grain
   macaroni
   (see Potpourri Procedures
   for how to cook pasta)
2½ c. PIMENTO CHEESE
   SAUCE

In skillet saute garlic in olive oil. Add onions and cook until soft. Put into bowl. Add remaining ingredients and stir together well. Pour into LECITHIN-OILED 8" x 8" baking dish. Cover and bake at 350° for 45-60 minutes.
YIELD: 5½ c. or 8" x 8" baking dish

MEATLESS ENTREES

BRAZIL NUT CASSEROLE

White Sauce:

2 c. SOY MILK
1 Tbs. cornstarch or 2 Tbs. whole wheat flour
1 Tbs. oil
1 tsp. salt
1 Tbs. onion powder
¼ tsp. garlic powder
1½ tsp. dried parsley
⅔ c. sliced black olives

⅔ c. sliced or chopped Brazil nuts (may use food processor)
3 c. cooked whole wheat or soy flat noodles (see Potpourri Procedure on how to cook whole grain pasta)

Blend first 6 ingredients briefly on high. Pour into medium saucepan and add dried parsley. Repeat recipe 1 more time. Cook white sauce on medium-high stirring constantly until thickened. Line bottom of LECITHIN-OILED 8" x 8" baking dish with ½ c. white sauce. Then layer with the following:

1½ c. cooked noodles
⅓ c. sliced olives
⅓ c. sliced brazil nuts
1½ c. white sauce

Repeat procedure ending with 1½ c. white sauce. Bake at 350° for 35-45 minutes.

YIELD: 8" x 8" baking dish

VEGETABLE STROGANOFF

3 c. fresh broccoli flowers and stalks cut into ⅛" slices
2 c. carrot circles, ⅛"
1 minced garlic clove
2 Tbs. olive oil
1 c. chopped onions

6 c. fresh sliced mushrooms
3 Tbs. whole wheat flour
3 c. SOY MILK
2 Tbs. soy sauce, unfermented
1 c. SOY SOUR CREAM

Steam first two ingredients separately until crisp-tender. Set aside. In skillet, briefly saute garlic in olive oil. Add next two ingredients and cook until soft. Remove from heat. Blend next three ingredients on high for 10 seconds. Pour into saucepan and cook over medium-high stirring constantly until thickened. Add vegetables and sour cream. Stir until heated through. Do not boil. Serve over whole wheat or soy flat noodles.

YIELD: 7 c.

MEATLESS ENTREES

CHICKPEA A LA KING

½ c. chopped onions
½ c. freshly sliced or canned mushrooms
2 Tbs. oil
2 Tbs. water
3 c. water and/or garbanzo liquid
½ c. cashew pieces
4 tsp. sesame seeds
3 Tbs. COUNTRY-STYLE SEASONING
¼ tsp. salt
¾ tsp. garlic powder
1 Tbs. onion powder
1 Tbs. cornstarch
2 c. frozen green peas
½ c. chopped pimentos
2 c. COOKED GARBANZOS (if salt free add ¼ tsp. salt)

Saute first two ingredients in oil and water until onions are clear. Set aside. Blend next eight ingredients on high 1-2 minutes until creamy. Pour into saucepan and cook over medium-high stirring constantly until thickened. Place peas in colander and rinse with hot water for 10-15 seconds. Add onions, peas and remaining ingredients to saucepan. Continue to stir while cooking for two more minutes. Serve over brown rice, flat noodles or toast.
YIELD: 7 c.

PERSIAN DILL RICE

4 c. frozen Fordhook lima beans
2 c. water
1⅛ tsp. salt
1 tsp. onion powder
½ tsp. garlic powder
1 Tbs. olive oil
3 c. COOKED BROWN RICE
1-2 Tbs. dill weed

Put first six ingredients in a pot. Bring to boil and simmer about 30 minutes until beans are tender. Drain beans and save juice. Line the bottom of 8" x 8" baking dish with 1¾ c. cooked Limas. Then layer with the following:
    1½ c. brown rice
    ½-1 Tbs. dill weed
    1¾ c. Limas
    1½ c. brown rice
Pour 1 c. juice from beans over rice. Next sprinkle on ½-1 Tbs. dill weed. Cover and bake at 350° for 45 minutes.
YIELD: 8" x 8" baking dish

MEATLESS ENTREES

ARMENIAN LENTIL PILAF

½ c. dry lentils	½ tsp. garlic powder
3 c. water	4 c. sliced onions
¾ c. bulgur or cracked wheat	⅓ c. olive oil
1½ tsp. salt	¾ c. water
2 tsp. onion powder	¼ tsp. salt

Put first two ingredients into pot and bring to boil. Reduce heat, cover and simmer until lentils are half cooked (about 20-25 minutes). Add bulgur and seasonings. Mix well. Cover and continue simmering until lentils are done and wheat absorbs all liquid (20-25 minutes). Put into LECITHIN-OILED 8" x 8" baking dish. Saute remaining ingredients on medium-high until onions are clear but not brown (about 20-25 minutes). Pour onions and liquid evenly over lentils. Cover with foil. Bake at 350° for 45 minutes.

YIELD: 6 c. or 8" x 8" baking dish

KIBBEE
(a Middle Eastern dish)

1 c. bulgur wheat	½ c. finely chopped celery
3 c. water	1½ tsp. salt
⅔ c. water	½ tsp. sage
¼ tsp. salt	½ tsp. oregano
½ c. regular rolled oats	½ tsp. garlic powder
2 minced garlic cloves	½ tsp. thyme
2 Tbs. olive oil	2 tsp. onion powder
½ c. chopped onions	2 Tbs. dried parsley
½ c. chopped green pepper	
½ c. chopped canned pimentos	

Soak bulgur in 3 c. water overnight. Next day in saucepan, bring ⅔ c. water and ¼ tsp. salt to boil. Stir several times to distribute salt. Add oats and reduce heat. Cover and simmer for 15-20 minutes. Remove from heat and put into bowl. Add bulgur and any remaining water from soaking. In skillet, saute garlic in olive oil. Add onions and pepper and cook until soft. Put into bowl along with remaining ingredients. Mix well with hands. Put into LECITHIN-OILED 8" x 8" baking dish. Bake at 350° for one hour.

YIELD: 6 c. or 8" x 8" baking dish

Variation: May add ½ c. COOKED GARBANZOS

STUFFED COURGETTES (Zucchini)

This is an excellent way to use large, overgrown zucchini or summer squash.

1 15" long zucchini (about 3½" in diameter)
5 c. KIBBEE (can be already baked)
1 recipe AIOLI

Wash and cut ends off zucchini. Cut in half lengthwise. Scoop out the center of each half, putting seeds and pulp into bowl. Add 5 c. KIBBEE to bowl and mix well with hands. Place zucchini on LECITHIN-OILED cookie sheet. Salt lightly and mound Kibbee in center of zucchini. Bake at 350° for 1 hour and 15 minutes or until almost tender. Remove from oven and top with AIOLI. Return to oven and bake 15 more minutes or until AIOLI is lightly browned.

VEGETABLE POT PIE

6 c. boiled potatoes, ½" cubes
2 c. carrot circles, ¼" thick
2 c. chopped onions
2 Tbs. olive oil
3 Tbs. water
1 c. frozen green peas
2 c. SOY MILK (omit vanilla and sweetener)
2 Tbs. whole wheat flour or cornstarch
3 Tbs. COUNTRY-STYLE SEASONING
1 Tbs. onion powder
¼ tsp. salt
1 tsp. yeast flakes
1 recipe FLAKY WHEAT-OAT PIE CRUST

Wash potatoes leaving on the skins. Boil in several inches of salted water until tender. Put potatoes in colander and rinse in cold water. Cool slightly and cut into chunks. Measure and put into bowl. Clean carrots and slice. In saucepan, steam in small amount of water until almost tender. Drain and add to potatoes. In skillet, saute onions in oil and water until soft. Add to bowl along with peas.

To make gravy: Blend next six ingredients briefly on high. Pour into saucepan. Make one more recipe of gravy and add to saucepan. Cook, stirring constantly on medium-high until thickened. Pour over vegetables in bowl. Gently mix everything together. Put into LECITHIN-OILED 9" x 13" baking dish. Top with pie crust, turning under edges and fluting. (see FLAKY WHEAT-OAT PIE CRUST for specific directions). Bake at 350° for one hour or until fluted edge is firm.

YIELD: 10 c. or 9" x 13" pot pie

Note: May also put crust on bottom.

MEATLESS ENTREES

SHEPHERD'S POT PIE

Make one recipe of HARVEST NUT ROAST. Do not bake but spread evenly into LECITHIN-OILED 9" x 13" baking dish. Make one recipe of EARLY MORNING POTATO PANCAKES, doubling milk and olive oil. Instead of forming into patties, spread on top of NUT ROAST. Cover with ½ c. SOY MAYONNAISE. May make a design on top with a knife. Sprinkle with paprika (optional). Bake at 350° for 60 minutes until mashed potatoes are golden.

YIELD: 9" x 13" baking dish

Note: For those who like mashed potatoes, make a double recipe of EARLY MORNING POTATO PANCAKES.

MEATLESS ENTREES

THE BEAN STORY

Beans are a nutritious, economical class of food, a rich source of carbohydrate, protein, fiber and other essential nutrients. But it is necessary to cook them thoroughly for the body to properly assimilate these important nutrients. It is helpful to know that some people cannot tolerate beans, for their digestive systems react unfavorably.

PREPARING BEANS FOR COOKING

Beans should first be sorted to remove any stones, sticks or off-colored beans. Then rinse well and soak 6 to 8 hours in plenty of water. (Use about 3 cups of water to every cup of beans for soaking). After soaking, drain beans. Use fresh water for cooking. See chart for amount of water to use for cooking. Add salt after beans are tender, otherwise cooking time will be increased. May squeeze lemon juice on cooked beans to aid in digestion.

VARIOUS COOKING METHODS FOR BEANS

1. In covered saucepan bring water and beans to a boil, reduce heat and simmer until tender. See following chart for cooking times.

2. Rinse, soak and drain beans. Place beans in crock pot. Use the following chart to determine how much water to use. Cook on high 6 to 8 hours. Some beans, like garbanzos and soybeans, may need to be cooked longer. Another option when using the crock pot is to not soak the beans first but to simply sort and rinse beans then put into crock pot. More water will be needed for cooking.

3. Pressure cooking is one of the quickest methods for tenderizing beans, especially garbanzos and soybeans. All beans, except split peas, may be soaked and pressure cooked at 5-10 lbs. for 30-120 minutes, depending on beans being used. See a pressure cooking book for the exact directions.

4. In covered saucepan bring beans and water to a boil. Pour into baking dish, cover. Bake at 300 for several hours until tender.

5. Instead of soaking for several hours bring beans and water to a boil in a covered saucepan. Then remove from heat and set aside for one hour. Drain water. Add fresh water using the following chart and cook until tender.

6. Handy home canned beans: Place 1⅔ c. washed and sorted dried beans or peas in a quart jar. (Do not soak beans.) May add 1 tsp. salt. Cover with water to within 1" of top of jar. Seal and process for 1½ hours at 10 lbs. pressure.

7. Soak beans, drain and freeze. Soaked beans are ready anytime to cook or to use soaked but uncooked in a recipe such as FLUFFY SOY-CORN MUFFIN.

MEATLESS ENTREES

COOKING TIME CHART FOR BEANS

(1 c. dry beans = approximately 2½ c. cooked)

Beans (Soaked)	Inches of Water to Cover Top of Beans	Approximate Cooking Time
Lentils, Split Peas, Mung Beans*	1″	1 hour
Black Beans, Kidney, Baby Lima, Pinto, Navy or White Beans	2″	2-3 hours
Garbanzo (Chick Peas), Soybeans	3″	4-5 hours

*No soaking required for this group

Amount of water may vary with beans as well as personal taste. Use more water for soup beans and less water for mashed or thick, creamy beans. Keep beans covered with water during cooking time. If necessary excess water may be drained off beans after cooking.

KIDNEY BEAN AND TOFU PIE

2 c. ½″ tofu cubes
2 minced garlic cloves
1½ Tbs. olive oil
1 c. chopped onions
1½ c. chopped celery
3 c. COOKED KIDNEY BEANS, drained

½ c. SOY MAYONNAISE
1 Tbs. onion powder
¾ tsp. salt
½ recipe FLAKY WHEAT-OAT PIE CRUST

Rinse, drain and cut tofu into cubes. Freeze overnight. Next day thaw. Soak tofu in soy sauce for 10 minutes. Drain. In skillet, saute garlic in olive oil. Add next two ingredients and cook until soft. Put into bowl and add next four ingredients along with marinated tofu. Mix together well. Put into LECITHIN-OILED 8″ x 8″ baking dish. Top with pie crust, turning under edges and fluting. May make design on top by pricking with fork. Bake at 350° for one hour or until fluted edge on crust is firm. (If using salt free beans use 1½ tsp. salt instead of ¾ tsp.)
YIELD: 6 c. or 8″ x 8″ baking dish

MEATLESS ENTREES

PASTY (pas'te)

(A traditional British pie filled with game, fish or the like. In place of the meat, we have used tofu.)

¾ lb.	frozen tofu (about 1¾ c.)	2 tsp.	onion powder
6 Tbs.	soy sauce, unfermented	1½ c.	chopped onions
2 tsp.	lemon juice	4 c.	½" raw potato cubes
1 Tbs.	olive oil	1 recipe	FLAKY WHEAT-OAT PIE
¼ tsp.	garlic powder		CRUST

Freeze tofu day before preparing this dish. Thaw and place in colander. Press out water. Break tofu into bite size chunks, about ½" pieces. Put into bowl. Add next six ingredients and mix together well. Add potatoes and stir. Make one recipe of pie crust. Roll out bottom crust. Place in oiled pie dish. Fill and cover with top crust, turning edge under and fluting. (see FLAKY WHEAT-OAT PIE CRUST for specific directions). Bake at 350° for one hour.

YIELD: 1 - 9" pie

SPINACH QUICHE

1 recipe	FLAKY WHEAT-OAT PIE CRUST	3 c.	PIMENTO CHEESE SAUCE
3 c.	frozen chopped spinach, cooked (packed into cup)		

Make one recipe pie crust. Roll out and flip into 10" quiche dish. Turn under and flute edges (see FLAKY WHEAT-OAT PIE CRUST for specific directions). After cooking spinach, put into colander and press out water firmly. Then measure, packing into cup. Line bottom of crust with spinach. Pour PIMENTO CHEESE SAUCE on top. Bake at 350° for 30 minutes.

YIELD: 1 - 10" quiche

Variations:

1. May use other greens such as kale or collards.
2. May substitute other vegetables in place of greens. Try combining sauteed onions, mushrooms or fresh tomato chunks.

MEATLESS ENTREES

CHILI

2 c. dry kidney beans (4 c. cooked)
2 minced garlic cloves
½ c. chopped onions
1 c. chopped green peppers
2 Tbs. olive oil
3 c. canned tomatoes with juice
1 Tbs. cumin

1 Tbs. paprika
1½ tsp. onion powder
¾ tsp. basil
½ tsp. garlic powder
2 tsp. salt
1½ tsp. honey
1 c. tomato paste

Soak beans overnight in a generous amount of water. Next day rinse and drain. Put into pot and cover with fresh water about two inches above beans. Bring to a boil. Reduce heat. Cover and simmer until tender. In another pot, saute next three ingredients in olive oil. Add canned tomatoes squashing with hands. Then add remaining ingredients and stir together well. When beans are tender, stir into tomato mixture. Simmer 45-60 minutes to blend flavors. Delicious with CORN BREAD.

YIELD: 8 c.

Note: When using tomatoes canned in puree, use 1 c. puree in place of paste.

QUICK & EASY CHILI

3 c. COOKED KIDNEY or PINTO BEANS

3 c. TOMATO SAUCE
2-3 Tbs. CHILI SEASONING

Put all ingredients into pot and stir together. Simmer for 30-45 minutes to blend flavors. Beans should be salt free.

YIELD: 5½ c.

RICH AND SAUCY BAKED BEANS

2½ c. dry navy beans
8 c. cooking water
1 minced garlic clove (optional)
2-3 Tbs. olive oil
1 c. chopped onions
3½ c. canned tomatoes measured with juice

½ c. tomato paste
¼ c. molasses
2 Tbs. honey
2 tsp. salt
1 tsp. basil or ITALIAN SEASONING

Continued on next page...

MEATLESS ENTREES

Soak beans in generous amount of water overnight. Next day drain and rinse. Put into pot and cover with 8 c. water. Bring to boil. Reduce heat, cover and simmer until tender (about 1½ hours). In skillet, briefly saute garlic in olive oil. Add onions and cook until soft. Set aside. When beans are tender, add onions and remaining ingredients to pot. Be sure to crush tomatoes with hands before adding. Stir together well. Pour into LECITHIN-OILED 9" x 13" baking dish. Bake at 350° for one hour. Cover and bake another 30 minutes.

YIELD: 11¾ c. or 9" x 13" baking dish

Note: If using canned tomatoes in puree, omit tomato paste and use 4½ c. canned tomatoes measured with puree.

HAYSTACKS

3 c. dry pinto beans	¾ tsp. garlic powder
7 c. water for cooking	1 Tbs. onion powder
2¼ tsp. salt	¾ tsp. cumin (or to taste)

Soak beans overnight in a generous amount of water. Next morning, rinse and drain beans. Put into pot and add 7 c. water. Bring to a boil, reduce heat, cover and simmer until beans are tender. May need to add more water. When beans are tender, add remaining ingredients and stir together well. Simmer several more minutes to blend flavors. Remove from heat and mash beans. Put into LECITHIN-OILED 8" x 8" baking dish. Bake at 350° for 20-30 minutes.

To serve: Place CORN CHIPS or CROUTONS on plate. Spoon beans on top. Then layer with the following: shredded lettuce, chopped tomatoes, finely diced onions, chopped black olives and PIMENTO CHEESE SAUCE. Delicious!

YIELD: 6 c. mashed beans or 8" x 8" baking dish

CORN CHIPS

To avoid the added oil in commercial corn chips, try this alternative. Brush uncooked tortillas with water and sprinkle with onion and/or garlic powder and salt. Place on cookie sheets and dry out in 225° oven. Break into pieces.

MEATLESS ENTREES

CUBAN BLACK BEANS

3 c. dry black beans
8 c. water for cooking
2 c. chopped onions
2 c. chopped green pepper
2-3 minced garlic cloves
3 Tbs. olive oil

3 Tbs. water
2 bay leaves
1 Tbs. salt
1 Tbs. onion powder
¾-1½ tsp. cumin (optional)
3 Tbs. lemon juice

Soak beans in generous amount of water overnight. In morning, rinse and drain beans. Put into pot with 8 c. water. Bring to boil, reduce heat, cover and simmer until beans are tender (about 3-4 hours). Saute next three ingredients in oil and water. When beans are tender, add sauteed vegetables along with remaining ingredients except lemon juice. Simmer 30 more minutes to blend flavors. Add lemon juice last. Serve over brown rice. May garnish with chopped scallions and tomato wedges.
YIELD: 9 c.

BOSTON BAKED BEANS

2½ c. dry navy beans
8 c. water for cooking
1¼ c. finely chopped onions
1 Tbs. oil
6-7 Tbs. dark molasses (not blackstrap)

1 Tbs. honey
2½ tsp. salt
1 Tbs. onion powder
½ tsp. garlic powder

Soak beans overnight in generous amount of water. Next morning, rinse and drain. Put soaked beans into pot with 8 c. water. Bring to boil. Reduce heat, cover and simmer until tender (about 1½ hours). Remove from heat. Saute onions in oil until clear. Add to beans along with remaining ingredients. Mix together well. Pour into LECITHIN-OILED 8" x 8" baking dish. Cover and bake at 350° for 2 hours. Uncover and bake for 30 more minutes.
YIELD: 9 c.

SIMPLE SAVORY LENTILS

2 c. dry lentils
8 c. water
2-3 minced garlic cloves
2 Tbs. olive oil

2½-3 tsp. savory
2 tsp. salt
2½ c. fresh chopped tomatoes
3 Tbs. tomato paste

Continued on next page...

MEATLESS ENTREES

In pot, bring first two ingredients to boil. Reduce heat to medium and cook uncovered until tender (about 30 minutes). In skillet, saute garlic in olive oil. When lentils are tender, add garlic and remaining ingredients. Simmer 20 more minutes to blend flavors.

YIELD: 8 c.

SOYBEAN CREOLE

4 minced garlic cloves	1½ tsp. salt
2 Tbs. olive oil	1 tsp. honey
3 Tbs. water	1 tsp. molasses (not blackstrap)
1 bay leaf	¾ c. bean liquid
¾ c. chopped onions	3 c. canned tomatoes
1 c. chopped green pepper	(measured with juice)
4 c. cooked, drained soybeans	½ c. tomato paste
(save liquid)	1 Tbs. dried parsley
1 Tbs. onion powder	
¾ tsp. ground thyme or 1½ tsp. leaf thyme	

In pot, saute garlic in olive oil. Add next four ingredients and cook until onions and peppers are soft. Add remaining ingredients and stir together well. Be sure to crush tomatoes with hands before adding. Simmer for 30 minutes to blend flavors and thicken.

YIELD: 7 c.

Note: If using tomatoes canned in puree, substitute tomato puree for paste.

PASTA E FAGIOLI

2 c. dry white beans	1 minced garlic clove
10 c. water	1 c. chopped onions
1 Tbs. salt	¼ c. fresh chopped parsley
2 stalks of celery with leaves	4 tsp. basil
¼ c. olive oil	2 c. dry whole grain macaroni

Continued on next page...

MEATLESS ENTREES

In pot, bring beans and water to boil. Simmer covered for 1 hour. Remove 4 c. of cooking water and put into another bowl. Blend 1 c. of beans with 1 c. of cooking water until smooth. Pour pureed beans back into pot. Repeat procedure with remaining 3 c. beans. Add salt and celery stalks to pot. Cover and simmer one hour. In skillet, saute garlic, onion, parsley and basil in olive oil. Cook for 5 minutes stirring constantly. Add to beans. Cover and cook for 30 minutes longer to blend flavors. Then stir in macaroni. Cook covered 15 more minutes. Remove and discard celery stalk.

YIELD: 8 c.

OATBURGERS

1½ c. chopped onions	1 tsp. oregano
2 Tbs. olive oil	2 tsp. ground dill seed
4½ c. water	⅓ c. yeast flakes
½ c. soy sauce, unfermented	½ c. sunflower seeds or
1½ tsp. garlic powder	chopped walnuts
1½ Tbs. onion powder	¾ c. cracked wheat
1½ tsp. basil	3½ c. regular rolled oats

In large pot, saute onions in olive oil until soft. Add remaining ingredients except oats. Stir together and boil 5 minutes. Add oats and mix briefly. Reduce heat and simmer 5 more minutes. Cover, set aside and let sit for 1 hour. Using ½ c. measure dipped into water, fill with oat mixture. Place on LECITHIN-OILED cookie sheet. To prevent sticking, dip hands into water before forming into burgers. Bake at 350° for 35 minutes. Turn over and bake an additional 15 minutes. Delicious served on whole grain bread or bun with lettuce, tomato, onion, KETCHUP or GOLDEN GARLIC MUSTARD. These burgers freeze well.

YIELD: 15 - ½ c. burgers

MEATLESS ENTREES

WALNUT-OLIVE BURGERS

1 c. black pitted olives	½ tsp. sage
¼ c. water	½ tsp. thyme
1 c. chopped walnuts	¼ tsp. marjoram
2½ c. regular rolled oats	½ tsp. garlic powder
1 c. finely chopped onions	½ tsp. onion powder
1 tsp. salt	1 c. walnuts
1 Tbs. soy sauce	1¾ c. water

Blend first two ingredients on high until smooth, stopping blender two or three times to stir contents. Pour into bowl and add next ten ingredients. Mix together. Blend last two ingredients on high for 1-2 minutes until creamy. Add to bowl and stir everything together well. Let sit for 15 minutes for oats to absorb liquid. Using ⅓ c. portions, place on LECITHIN-OILED cookie sheet and form into burgers. Bake at 350° for 20 minutes on each side.

YIELD: 13 - ⅓ c. burgers

Variation: To accompany a fruit meal, omit chopped onions and add 1 Tbs. onion powder.

BARLEY BURGERS

3 c. water	1 Tbs. onion powder
½ c. pearled barley	½ tsp. garlic powder
1 tsp. salt	1 tsp. salt
½ c. chopped onion	¼ tsp. thyme
2 Tbs. olive oil	¼ tsp. sage
3 Tbs. water	¼ tsp. savory
½ c. chopped walnuts	1 c. SOY MILK
1 c. shredded raw potatoes	2 c. whole grain BREAD
(2 medium)	CRUMBS

In saucepan bring first three ingredients to boil. Reduce heat, cover and simmer until water is absorbed (about 1 hour). While barley is cooking, in skillet saute onions in olive oil and water until soft. Then put cooked barley, sauteed onions and remaining ingredients in bowl and stir together well. Using ½ c. portions, form into burgers and place on LECITHIN-OILED cookie sheet. Bake at 350° for 30 minutes. Turn over and bake 15 more minutes.

YIELD: 16 - ⅓ c. burgers

MEATLESS ENTREES

SUNBURGER PATTIES

2 c. grated carrots
2 c. sunflower seeds
½ c. chopped onion
2 Tbs. water

1¼ c. tomato juice
1½ tsp. salt
1 Tbs. onion powder

Clean, grate and measure carrots; put in bowl. Grind sunflower seeds in blender or food processor until fine (3 c. ground). Add to carrots. In skillet saute onions in water until soft. Add to bowl along with remaining ingredients. Stir together well. Using ⅓ c. portions, place on LECITHIN-OILED cookie sheet and form into patties. Bake at 350° for 35 minutes. Turn over and bake an additional 15 minutes.

YIELD: 10 - ⅓ c. patties

SUNSHINE TIMBALES

4½ c. COOKED LONG GRAIN
    BROWN RICE (1½ c. dry)
1½ Tbs. soy oil
⅓ c. chopped onions
⅓ c. chopped celery
½ c. ground sunflower seeds
⅓ c. chopped walnuts
3 Tbs. COUNTRY-STYLE
    SEASONING

3 Tbs. dried parsley
1½ tsp. onion powder
½ tsp. garlic powder
½ tsp. savory
1¼ c. whole grain BREAD
    CRUMBS

Cook rice the day before. Chill overnight covered. Next day, measure and put in bowl. In skillet, saute onions in oil. Drain off liquid. Add onions to bowl along with remaining ingredients except BREAD CRUMBS. Mix well with hands. Using ⅓ c. portions, form into balls pressing together firmly. Drop balls into bread crumbs and cover thoroughly. Place ball onto LECITHIN-OILED cookie sheet. Bake at 350° for 40 minutes. Delicious served with CASHEW WHITE SAUCE.

YIELD: 16 - ⅓ c. balls

CASHEW WHITE SAUCE

1 c. cashew pieces
1½ c. water
2 Tbs. onion powder
¼ tsp. garlic powder

1½ tsp. salt
2½ c. water
1 Tbs. dried parsley

Continued on next page...

MEATLESS ENTREES

...

Blend first five ingredients on high 1-2 minutes until creamy. While blender is running, pour in remaining 2½ c. water and blend briefly. Pour into saucepan and add parsley. Cook over medium-high stirring constantly until thickened. Delicious over SUNSHINE TIMBALES.

YIELD: 4 c.

BRAZIL NUT BALLS

1 c. grated onions	2 Tbs. onion powder
1 Tbs. basil	2 Tbs. soy sauce, unfermented
1-2 Tbs. olive oil	2 c. Brazil nuts
1 c. SOY MILK	4 c. whole grain BREAD
1¼ tsp. salt	CRUMBS
1½ tsp. garlic powder	

In skillet, saute onions and basil in olive oil until onions are soft. Put into bowl and add next five ingredients. Grind brazil nuts ½ c. at a time in blender until fine. Add to bowl along with BREAD CRUMBS. Stir together well. Form into ⅛ c. (2 Tbs.) balls and place on LECITHIN-OILED cookie sheet. Bake at 350° for 20 minutes. Turn over bake 15 more minutes.

YIELD: 39 - ⅛ c. (2 Tbs.) balls

Variation: May make into burgers.

YIELD: 14 - ⅓ c. burgers. Bake at 350° for 20 minutes. Turn over and bake an additional 10 minutes.

OATBURGER BALLS

Make 1 recipe OATBURGERS. To make into balls, use ¼ c. measure dipped into water. Fill with oat mixture. To prevent sticking, dip hands into water before removing oat mixture and forming balls. Place on LECITHIN-OILED cookie sheet. Bake at 350° for 40 minutes.

YIELD: 30 - ¼ c. balls.

MEATLESS ENTREES

TOFU BALLS

6 c. crumbled tofu
2 c. whole grain BREAD
CRUMBS
2 Tbs. onion powder
1 tsp. garlic powder

1 Tbs. oregano
1 Tbs. basil
1¼ tsp. salt
1 c. PIMENTO CHEESE
SAUCE

Rinse, drain, crumble and measure tofu. Put into bowl and add remaining ingredients. Mix together well. Form into ⅛ c. (2 Tbs.) balls. Place on LECITHIN-OILED cookie sheet. Cover with foil. Bake at 350° for 45 minutes. Uncover and bake an additional 10-15 minutes to brown.
YIELD: 40 - ⅛ c. (2 Tbs.) balls

TOMATO SAUCE

4 minced garlic cloves
2-3 Tbs. olive oil
1½ c. chopped onions
¾ c. chopped green pepper
(optional)
4 c. canned tomatoes with
juice

1 c. tomato paste
2 tsp. basil
1 tsp. oregano (leaf)
1 tsp. salt
1 Tbs. honey

In pot, saute garlic in olive oil. Add onions and peppers and saute until soft. Add tomatoes, squashing with hands. Add remaining ingredients. Stir together. Simmer for an hour to blend flavors. Freezes well.
YIELD: 6 c.
Variations:
1. In place on honey, may add 1-2 c. finely shredded carrots. Simmer in sauce for 30 minutes. Carrots are not seen, but add flavor and sweetness.
2. For garlic lovers, may add minced garlic 15 minutes before end of cooking.
Note: When using tomatoes canned in puree, substitute puree for paste.

SPAGHETTI AND NO-MEAT BALLS

Cook whole grain spaghetti (see POTPOURRI PROCEDURES for how to cook whole grain pasta). When drained, toss lightly in olive oil. May add dried parsley. Make TOMATO SAUCE and one of the following no-meat balls: OATBURGER, BRAZIL NUT or TOFU. Prepare PIMENTO CHEESE SAUCE. Serve each item in separate bowl. Delicious with garlic bread.

MEATLESS ENTREES

LASAGNE

2 c. crumbled tofu
¾ tsp. salt
1¼ tsp. onion powder
¼ tsp. garlic powder
7½ c. TOMATO SAUCE

2½ c. PIMENTO CHEESE SAUCE
16 whole grain lasagne noodles

Rinse, drain, crumble and measure tofu. Put into bowl and add next three ingredients. Mix together well with hands. Line the bottom of LECITHIN-OILED 9" x 13" baking dish with 1½ c. TOMATO SAUCE. Then layer with the following:

4 uncovered lasagne noodles slightly overlapping (may have to break noodles to fit length of dish)
2½ c. TOMATO SAUCE
4 lasagne noodles
¾ c. seasoned tofu
¾ c. PIMENTO CHEESE
4 lasagne noodles
¾ c. seasoned tofu
¾ c. PIMENTO CHEESE
4 lasagne noodles
3½ c. TOMATO SAUCE

Use remaining PIMENTO CHEESE and tofu to decorate top. Bake at 350° for one hour. Cover and bake an additional 20-30 minutes.
YIELD: 9" x 13" baking dish

STUFFED SHELLS

3 c. tofu
2 c. SOY MAYONNAISE or SOY SOUR CREAM
2 Tbs. basil
2 Tbs. oregano

2 Tbs. onion powder
1 Tbs. garlic powder
2 tsp. salt
20 Manicotti shells
4 c. TOMATO SAUCE

Rinse, drain, mash and measure tofu. Put tofu in bowl with next six items. Mix well. Fill half COOKED SHELLS with ¼ c. of the tofu cheese mixture. Line bottom of LECITHIN-OILED 9" x 13" baking dish with 1 c. TOMATO SAUCE. Place stuffed shells on sauce. Cover shells with remaining 3 c. of sauce. Bake at 350° for 60 minutes. For added eye appeal add enough water to some extra SOY MAYONNAISE or SOUR CREAM to dribble over dish to make attractive design. This should be done after dish has baked 45 minutes. The topping will turn light golden brown during last 15 minutes of baking.
YIELD: 20 stuffed shells

MEATLESS ENTREES

EGGPLANT PARMESAN

2 large eggplants (about
   3 lbs.)
   BREADING MEAL
2 c. crumbled tofu
¾ tsp. salt

1¼ tsp. onion powder
¼ tsp. garlic powder
7 c. TOMATO SAUCE
2 c. PIMENTO CHEESE
   SAUCE

Cut ends off eggplant and slice into circles ½" thick. Dip slices into water then coat in BREADING MEAL. Place on LECITHIN-OILED cookie sheet. Bake at 350° for 15 minutes. Turn eggplant slices over and bake 10-15 more minutes until tender and browned. While eggplant is baking, rinse, drain, crumble and measure tofu. Put into bowl and add next three ingredients. Mix together well with hands. When eggplant is tender, line the bottom of LECITHIN-OILED 9" x 13" baking dish with 1 c. TOMATO SAUCE. Then layer with following:

   baked eggplant slightly overlapping
   ½ c. seasoned tofu
   ⅓ c. PIMENTO CHEESE SAUCE
   2 c. TOMATO SAUCE

Repeat procedure two more times, ending with 2 c. TOMATO SAUCE. After second layer, press down firmly on eggplant to make room for next layer. Decorate top with remaining PIMENTO CHEESE and tofu. Bake at 350° for 1 hour.

YIELD: 9" x 13" baking dish

BREADING MEAL

2 c. whole wheat flour
1 c. yeast flakes
1 Tbs. salt

½ c. dried parsley
1 Tbs. garlic powder
1 c. cornmeal

Put all ingredients in bowl and stir together well. Store in airtight container.

YIELD: 4½ c.

MEATLESS ENTREES

TOFU CACCIATORE

4 c. ¼" x 1" x 2" tofu strips
2 c. water
¼ tsp. tarragon
½ tsp. thyme
½ tsp. marjoram
½ tsp. basil
2 bay leaves

1 c. chopped onions
1 c. fresh sliced mushrooms
¼ c. minced fresh garlic
¼ c. olive oil
1½ tsp. salt
1½ c. tomato puree

Rinse, drain and cut tofu into strips. In saucepan, boil tofu in water uncovered for 15 minutes. Allow water to boil away as rest of ingredients are added in order given. Most of water should be gone when tomato puree is added. Stir together. Cover and simmer slowly 10-15 minutes. Serve over pasta, brown rice or millet.
YIELD: 6 c.

STUFFED PEPPERS

½ recipe ARMENIAN LENTIL
PILAF, omitting onions
for top
¾ c. canned, drained tomatoes

1 Tbs. olive oil
1 Tbs. water
½ c. chopped onions

Sauce:
1¾ c. water
1¾ c. tomato puree
3 Tbs. olive oil
2 Tbs. honey
1 Tbs. + 1 tsp. ITALIAN SEASONING
2 Tbs. onion powder
1½ tsp. garlic powder
½ tsp. cumin
2½ tsp. salt
5 medium green peppers
½ recipe PIMENTO CHEESE SAUCE

In pot, prepare ARMENIAN LENTIL PILAF. When lentils and bulgur are cooked, remove from heat. Add canned tomatoes to pot, crushing with hands. In skillet, saute onions in olive oil and water until soft. Add to PILAF and stir together well. Set aside.

Continued on next page...

To make sauce: Put next nine ingredients into saucepan. Bring to boil. Reduce heat, cover and simmer 30 minutes to blend flavors. While sauce is cooking, wash peppers and cut in half lengthwise. Remove stems, seeds and membranes. Slightly mound 9 pepper halves with Pilaf. (There will be ½ pepper remaining.) When sauce is cooked, pour into LECITHIN-OILED 9" x 13" baking dish. Place stuffed peppers into sauce. Spoon small amount of sauce over each pepper. Bake at 350° for one hour. Remove from oven and pour PIMENTO CHEESE over peppers. Bake an additional 15 minutes.
YIELD: 9 medium stuffed peppers or 9" x 13" baking dish

PIZZA

1 recipe **FLAKY WHEAT-OAT PIE CRUST**	1 c. **crumbled tofu (optional)**
3-4 c. **TOMATO SAUCE**	1½-2 c. **PIMENTO CHEESE SAUCE or LESSARELLA CHEEZ**
thinly sliced onions, pepper or olives (optional)	

Make one recipe pie crust. Roll out and flip onto 13¼" round pizza pan. Turn under edges and flute (see FLAKY WHEAT-OAT PIE CRUST (for specific directions). Bake at 350° for 15-20 minutes. Remove from oven and line with TOMATO SAUCE. May add vegetables of your choice and/or tofu. Pour on PIMENTO CHEESE and bake at 350° for 30-45 minutes.
YIELD: 1 - 13¼" round pizza

ENCHILADAS!

ENCHILADA SAUCE

7 **minced garlic cloves**	4-6 Tbs. **CHILI SEASONING**
2 Tbs. **olive oil**	1¾ tsp. **salt**
1 c. **chopped onions**	1 Tbs. **honey**
6 c. **canned tomatoes in puree (measured with puree)**	

In saucepan saute garlic and onions. Add canned tomatoes, crushing with hands, and remaining ingredients. Bring to boil. Reduce heat, cover and simmer for 20 minutes to blend flavors.
YIELD: 6¾ c.

MEATLESS ENTREES

CHILI SEASONING

¼ c. paprika
¼ c. cumin
1½ Tbs. ITALIAN SEASONING

1½ Tbs. oregano
3 Tbs. garlic powder
1 tsp. turmeric

Blend all ingredients on high until fine, stopping blender 2-3 times to stir. Store in airtight container.
YIELD: ¾ c.

ENCHILADA FILLING

4 c. COOKED PINTO BEANS, drained
¾ tsp. salt
2 tsp. onion powder

¾ tsp. garlic powder
¾ tsp. cumin
½ c. tomato puree

Put beans into bowl and partially mash. Add remaining ingredients and mix together mix. (If using salt free beans use 1¾ tsp. salt instead of ¾ tsp.)
YIELD: 3½ c.

To assemble enchiladas:
    8 - 6" tortillas
    3¾ c. ENCHILADA SAUCE
    2⅔ c. ENCHILADA FILLING
    1 c. PIMENTO CHEESE SAUCE
    ⅔ c. finely chopped onions
    ½ c. chopped black olives

Line bottom of LECITHIN-OILED 9" x 13" baking dish with ¾ c. SAUCE. Spread ⅓ c. of FILLING down center of one tortilla. Roll up and place seam down lengthwise in baking dish. Repeat procedure with remaining tortillas ending with two rows of four. On top of center of each row, layer with the following:
    1½ c. SAUCE
    ½ c. PIMENTO CHEESE
    ⅓ c. onions
    ¼ c. olives

Bake at 350° for 20-25 minutes.
YIELD: 8 enchiladas

MEATLESS ENTREES

THE VALUE OF A POTATO

Contrary to popular opinion, potatoes are NOT fattening; it is what you put on the potato that adds all the fat – butter, margarine, sour cream, gravy, etc. The potato is a most wonderful food; besides being delicious, it is a nutritional prize. Potatoes are a marvelous source of complex carbo-hydrate, a fair source of protein and dietary fiber. They also provide a bit of calcium, iron and niacin. Potatoes are a good source of thiamine (B1) and riboflavin (B2) and phosphorous. But they are an excellent source of potassium. One 2½" baked potato contains 503 mg.! And did you know that that same potato also provides 20 mg. of Vitamin C.* Be careful though — don't peel that skin off. Many of these precious nutrients are right under the skin. Besides, the skin of a baked potato is a crunch taste treat. With all that to offer, it's time to take the potato off the side dish and put it on the main plate as the star attraction. That's why we've put the next two entree suggestions in our cookbook. We don't want you to ever feel embarrassed about offering potatoes for the main course of your meal. In fact, eat them and enjoy. Bon Appétit!

*Food Values of Portions Commonly Used, Bowes and Church, Eleventh Edition.

CREATE-A-POTATO

Wash the skins on baking potatoes well. Prick twice and place on oven racks (may wrap in foil). Bake at 400° until fork slides easily into center (about 1½-2 hours). Serve with your choice of the following topping suggestions:

- olive oil
- yeast flakes
- AIOLI
- SOY SOUR CREAM
- PIMENTO CHEESE SAUCE
- sauteed onions
- sauteed mushrooms
- COUNTRY STYLE GRAVY
- KETCHUP
- ENCHILADA SAUCE
- chopped olives
- SCRAMBLED TOFU
- TAHINI MAYONNAISE
- CUCUMBER DRESSING
- OLIVE DRESSING
- POTTAGE DU FROMAGE
- CHEEZY BROCCOLI SOUP

Use your imagination for other topping creations.

MEATLESS ENTREES

MUSHROOM MOUNTAINS

Prepare and bake potatoes (see "Create-a-Potato"). While potatoes are baking, in one skillet saute fresh sliced mushrooms in small amount of olive oil. May season to taste with onion and/or garlic powder and salt. In another skillet, saute fresh sliced onions in the same manner as mushrooms. Make SOY SOUR CREAM. To serve: Arrange lettuce attractively on platter. Place baked potatoes on lettuce. Cut lengthwise in center and push ends to open up. Put a generous amount of sauteed mushroom and onions inside each potato. Top with a dollop of SOY SOUR CREAM and a sprinkle of paprika. Scrumptious!

CHEESY SCALLOPED POTATOES

8 c. thinly sliced raw potatoes (⅛" thick)	3 recipes PIMENTO CHEESE SAUCE
4 c. thinly sliced onions (⅛" thick)	

Line the bottom of LECITHIN-OILED 9" x 13" baking dish with 1 c. PIMENTO CHEESE. Then layer with the following:

    4 c. sliced potatoes
    salt to taste
    2 c. sliced onions
    3 c. PIMENTO CHEESE

Repeat procedure ending with 3 c. PIMENTO CHEESE SAUCE. Cover and bake at 400° for 1½ hours.

YIELD: 9" x 13" baking dish.

Where is Provence?
What does the word Provencale mean?

Provence is a region in Southeastern France bordering on the Mediterranean. Provencale (pro/ven sal') is an adjective referring to the cookery from this region which is characterized by the use of fresh garlic, olive oil, herbs and vegetables. The herbs are also called aromatic because they yield a fragrant smell when growing as when dried. Provence is world famous for the cultivation of such wonderful herbs as basil, oregano, marjoram, sage, thyme, rosemary and savory.

All recipes bearing the name Provencale are adaptations from our Country Life, Paris Restaurant. Several of the family there lived for years on a farm in Provence, where, among other things, they mastered the delightful cookery of the region. We hope you enjoy it too.

MEATLESS ENTREES

POTATOES PROVENCALE

2 c. coarsely chopped onions
4 c. thinly sliced (⅛") raw potatoes (with skins)
20 tomato slices, ¼" thick (about 4 medium tomatoes)

½ recipe AIOLI
4 tsp. HERBES DE PROVENCE

Line the bottom of LECITHIN-OILED 8" x 8" baking dish with 1 c. chopped onions. Then layer with the following:
2 c. sliced potatoes
salt to taste
⅓ -½ c. AIOLI
10 tomato slices
2 tsp. HERBES DE PROVENCE
Repeat procedure again ending with herbs. Cover and bake at 400° for 1¼ hours.
YIELD: 8" x 8" baking dish

HERBES DE PROVENCE

1 Tbs. marjoram or sage
1 Tbs. thyme
1 Tbs. basil

1 Tbs. rosemary
1 Tbs. savory

Put all into bowl and mix together well. Do not use ground herbs.
YIELD: 5 Tbs.

RATATOUILLE PROVENCALE

1 c. sliced onions
3 c. ¾" eggplant cubes
¼ c. olive oil
4 c. ¾" zucchini cubes
½ c. coarsely chopped green pepper (⅜" squares)
1½ tsp. salt

3 Tbs. water
¼ c. tomato puree
¾ tsp. basil
1 bay leaf
1½ tsp. HERBES DE PROVENCE
2 minced garlic cloves
3 c. ¾" tomato chunks

Continued on next page...

In large skillet, saute first two ingredients in olive oil until eggplant is slightly browned and tender on outside (about 10 minutes). Stir often. Add next eight ingredients and stir together. Cover and cook until zucchini is half done (about 30 minutes). Stir occasionally. Add garlic. Cover and cook until zucchini and eggplant are tender. Add tomatoes and cook briefly until soft. Remove bay leaves and serve.

YIELD: 6 c.

TOMATO SAUCE PROVENCALE

2 c. coarsely chopped onions	¼ tsp. rosemary
¼ c. olive oil	¼ tsp. thyme
4 minced garlic cloves	1 tsp. garlic powder
8 c. tomatoes canned in puree	1 Tbs. honey
2 bay leaves	1 tsp. salt
2 tsp. basil	

Saute onions in olive oil on medium-high for 20 minutes. Stir occasionally. Reduce heat, cover and continue to cook until golden brown. Uncover. Add garlic and cook for 2-3 minutes. Then add tomatoes, crushing with hands, and next five ingredients. Simmer for an hour. Add honey and salt. Simmer 5 minutes more. A satisfying change from our usual favorite TOMATO SAUCE.

YIELD: 9 c.

PIZZA PROVENCALE

1 recipe FLAKY WHEAT-OAT PIE CRUST	1½ tsp. thyme
6 c. chopped onions	1½ tsp. savory
3 Tbs. olive oil	2¼ tsp. oregano
1½ tsp. salt	2¼ tsp. basil
24 tomato slices, ¼" thick (about 5 medium tomatoes)	2 tsp. olive oil
	1 c. pitted black olives
	1 recipe AIOLI

Continued on next page...

MEATLESS ENTREES

TOFU FOO YOUNG

2 c. tofu, packed into cup
2 c. water
1 c. quick oats
2 Tbs. cornstarch
2 Tbs. oil
2 tsp. salt
¼ c. yeast flakes
½ tsp. turmeric or ¼ c. cooked
  or raw carrots
1 Tbs. onion powder

1 tsp. thyme
¼ tsp. garlic powder
1 Tbs. dried parsley
1 - 6 oz. box frozen snow peas
  (1 c.)
3 c. very thinly sliced white
  cabbage strips
2 c. fresh sliced mushrooms
2 c. very thinly sliced onions
¼ c. finely chopped parsley

Rinse, drain and measure tofu, breaking into cup. Put into blender and add next 11 ingredients. Blend on high until creamy, stopping blender two or three times to stir contents. Put into bowl and add remaining ingredients and mix together. Using ½ c. portions, drop onto LECITHIN-OILED cookie sheet, leaving 2″ between patties. Bake at 350° for 30 minutes. Remove from oven and allow to sit for 5 minutes before removing from cookie sheet. Serve with ORIENTAL MUSHROOM GRAVY.

YIELD: 16 patties

Note: These may also be cooked in a non-stick coated skillet until lightly browned on both sides.

FRIED RICE

2½ c. water
½ tsp. salt
1¼ c. DEXTRINIZED long grain
  brown rice
1½ Tbs. soy oil
2 Tbs. water
2 c. chopped onions
2 c. chopped celery
1-2 minced garlic cloves

1 Tbs. soy oil
3 c. fresh sliced mushrooms
2 Tbs. water
¼ c. soy sauce, unfermented
½ tsp. salt
1-2 Tbs. sesame oil
2 c. SCRAMBLED TOFU (omit
  onions)
½ c. chopped scallions

In saucepan bring first two ingredients to boil. Stir several times to distribute salt. Add rice and bring to boil again. Reduce heat, cover and simmer until water is absorbed (about 45 minutes). DO NOT STIR or rice will become mushy. Remove from heat and let sit covered for 20 minutes. Then put cooked rice into covered container and chill for an hour before proceeding with recipe. May also cook rice the day before and chill

Continued on next page...

MEATLESS ENTREES

overnight. When rice is thoroughly cooled, put 1½ Tbs. oil and 2 Tbs. water in large skillet (12"). Add onions and celery, sauteing on opposite sides of skillet on medium-high until half cooked. In another skillet, saute garlic in 1 Tbs. oil. Add mushrooms and 2 Tbs. water. Cover and simmer until mushrooms are soft. Then add celery along with cooked rice and remaining ingredients except scallions. Stir and cook everything together on medium-high for 10 minutes until flavors are blended and rice is hot. Now add scallions. Cook for one more minute. Serve. Scrumptious!
YIELD: 7½ c.

ORIENTAL MEDLEY

1 c. frozen snow peas (packed into cup)	2 c. water
	1½ tsp. salt
1 c. frozen chopped spinach	1 recipe ORIENTAL MUSHROOM
4 c. ½" tofu cubes	GRAVY

If using frozen vegetables, thaw and then measure. Put snow peas and greens in pot. Rinse, drain and cube tofu. Add it to vegetables along with water and salt. Boil all together for 5 minutes. Remove from heat and drain off water. Add hot MUSHROOM GRAVY and stir together gently. Serve over brown rice or toast.
YIELD: 8 c.
Note: May use other greens, fresh or frozen, but cook them first.

ORIENTAL MUSHROOM GRAVY

4 c. water	1½ c. finely chopped fresh mushrooms
6 Tbs. soy sauce, unfermented	
5 Tbs. cornstarch	¼ tsp. salt

Briefly blend on high first three ingredients. Pour into saucepan and add mushrooms. Cook, stirring constantly, over medium-high until thickened.
YIELD: 4 c.

MEATLESS ENTREES

—————— COUNTRY-STYLE SEASONING —

1⅓ c. yeast flakes	½ tsp. turmeric
1 Tbs. onion powder	1 tsp. dried parsley
2 tsp. garlic powder	1 Tbs. barley malt powder,
1 Tbs. paprika	optional
½ tsp. ground celery seed	3 Tbs. salt

Blend all ingredients on high until fine. Let sit in covered blender 2-3 minutes before removing. Store in covered container. Do not need to refrigerate.

YIELD: ¾ c.

———————— ITALIAN SEASONING ————————

What do you do when a recipe calls for Italian Seasoning and you don't have any? Do you choose another recipe or run to the store? Now you can save time and expense. Just put the following six herbs into a bowl and mix together well. In less than one minute, you have created your own Italian Seasoning. And the price is certainly right.

1 Tbs. basil	1 Tbs. thyme
1 Tbs. oregano	1 Tbs. rosemary
1 Tbs. marjoram or sage	1 Tbs. savory

Store in airtight container. Do not use ground herbs. If you're missing an herb or two, don't let that discourage you. Just use what you have.

YIELD: 6 Tbs.

———— TOASTED "CHEESE" SANDWICHES ————

1 c. water	¼ tsp. ground dill seed (optional)
¾ c. cashew pieces	3 Tbs. yeast flakes
2 Tbs. sesame seeds (optional)	½ c. pimentos
1¼ tsp. salt	1-2 Tbs. lemon juice
¼ tsp. garlic powder	¼ c. regular rolled or quick
2 tsp. onion powder	oats

Blend all ingredients on high 1-3 minutes until creamy. Pour into saucepan. Cook over medium-high stirring constantly until thickened. Make "cheese" sandwiches with whole grain bread. May add SOY MAYONNAISE, and sliced tomato.

YIELD: 2 c.

MEATLESS ENTREES

LENTIL COLD CUTS

1½ c. finely diced onions	3 Tbs. yeast flakes
2 Tbs. olive oil	¾ tsp. celery seed
1½ c. dry lentils	¼ tsp. sage
3½ c. water	1½ tsp. basil
2 tsp. salt	¼ tsp. cumin
2 tsp. soy sauce, unfermented	2 tsp. garlic powder

In saucepan saute onions in oil. Grind lentils fine in blender, stopping blender two or three times to stir contents. Add to saucepan along with remaining ingredients. Boil 5 minutes stirring constantly. Reduce heat, cover and simmer for one hour. Put into medium loaf pan and chill for several hours or until firm. To serve: invert on plate and slice. Makes delicious sandwiches with lettuce, tomato and SOY MAYONNAISE.

YIELD: 5 c. or 1 medium loaf pan (8½" x 4½" x 2½")

BEAN SPREAD

4 c. COOKED BEANS, drained (kidney or pinto are best)	⅔ c. SOY MAYONNAISE
	1-1½ tsp. onion powder
	½ tsp. garlic powder
1½ c. chopped celery	

Put beans into bowl and mash well. Add remaining ingredients and mix together. Makes a delicious sandwich with lettuce and tomato. If using salt free beans add 1 tsp. salt.

YIELD: 4 c.

Variation: May add fresh chopped onions to taste.

WALNUT CHEESE SPREAD

1 c. tofu, packed into cup	1¼ tsp. onion powder
¼ c. finely chopped walnuts	⅛ tsp. garlic powder
⅔ c. finely chopped black olives	½ tsp. salt
	½ c. SOY MAYONNAISE
3 Tbs. finely chopped celery	

Rinse, drain, measure tofu, packing into cup. Put into bowl and add remaining ingredients. Stir together well.

YIELD: 2 c.

MEATLESS ENTREES

GLUTEN

This recipe for making GLUTEN is presented with two separate methods. For those who have a bread mixing machine see method #1. For those mixing by hand see method #2. Also note that there are three different recipes for using the gluten — SHISH KABOBS, HAWAIIAN BBQ AND PEPPER STEAKS. A broth for cooking the gluten in is always necessary before making one of these three recipes. There are two broths given here to choose from: BROTH #1 and BROTH #2.

GLUTEN #1
(For use with bread machine)

⅓ c. walnuts	1 tsp. onion powder
¼ c. rolled oats	½ tsp. garlic powder
½ c. yeast flakes	1¾ c. warm water
1 tsp. salt	2½ c. gluten flour

Blend first seven ingredients on high until creamy, approximately 30 seconds. Place blended mixture into mixing bowl of bread machine. Use dough hook. Set at low add all flour. Mix for several minutes until it forms a rubber-like ball. Remove dough. Cut to desired size depending on entree being used. Do not stack pieces while cutting, as they will stick together. Bring BROTH #1 or #2 to a boil in a covered sauce pan. Drop pieces into boiling broth. Lightly boil 1-2 hours. Cook until done or soft throughout.

YIELD: 2 quarts gluten pieces.

GLUTEN #2
(For mixing by hand)

1½ c. walnuts	½ tsp. garlic powder
¼ c. rolled oats	1 c. whole wheat flour
¼ c. yeast flakes	2 c. cold water
1 tsp. onion powder	2 c. gluten flour

Blend walnuts and oats on high until ground. Pour into bowl and add flours and seasonings. Add cold water and quickly knead. Cut into desired shape depending on which entree will be used or roll into a log shape, about 2" in diameter. Cut into ¾" slices and drop into boiling BROTH #1 or #2. Lightly boil 1-2 hours until done or soft throughout.

YIELD: 2 quarts gluten pieces.

Continued

MEATLESS ENTREES

BROTH #1

10 c. water	1¾ tsp. thyme
⅓ c. soy sauce, unfermented	1¼ tsp. oregano
1¼ tsp. salt	2½ c. sliced onions
½ tsp. sage, powder	

Stir together well all ingredients in sauce pan.
YIELD: 11-12 cups

BROTH #2

10 c. water	¼ c. yeast flakes
½ c. soy sauce, unfermented	½ tsp. celery seed
1½ tsp. salt	½ tsp. ITALIAN SEASONING
1½ tsp. onion powder	1 Tbs. soy oil
1½ tsp. garlic powder	1 tsp. sweet basil
2 tsp. COUNTRY-STYLE SEASONING	2 bay leaves
	1 c. chopped onions

Stir together well all ingredients in sauce pan.
YIELD: 11-12 cups

SHISH KABOBS

After gluten has been kneaded cut one recipe into pieces, 1½" x ½". Boil in broth until done (see gluten procedure). Remove from broth and let cool. Soak in TERIYAKI SAUCE for 10 to 20 minutes. Place pieces on oiled cookie sheet (use olive or soy oil). Lightly spray or baste more of the same oil on top of each piece. Bake at 350° for 20 minutes. Turn over and bake 5 more minutes or until edges are crisp and brown. Watch carefully.

Procedure to making Kabobs:

Cut onions and green peppers in 1" squares. Rinse cherry tomatoes. Place on kabob skewers in the following order:

> gluten
> onion
> tomato
> pepper
> pineapple chunk, optional

Repeat until skewer is almost full. End with whole mushroom.

Place skewers on oiled cookie sheet. Pour KABOB SAUCE over them. Bake at 350° until vegetables are lightly cooked and still crispy, roximately 5-7 minutes. Watch carefully.

Continued on next page...

MEATLESS ENTREES

TERIYAKI SAUCE

2 c. soy sauce, unfermented
½ c. lemon juice
½ c. water

1½ Tbs. onion powder
1 tsp. garlic powder
½ c. honey

Mix well together in a bowl.
YIELD: 7 cups

KABOB SAUCE

1½ c. tomato puree
2 Tbs. lemon juice
3 Tbs. soy sauce, unfermented

2 Tbs. honey
⅛ tsp. garlic powder
2 Tbs. pineapple juice

Mix well together in a bowl.
YIELD: 2 cups

HAWAIIAN BBQ

After gluten has been kneaded cut one recipe into pieces, 2" x 1" x ½". Boil in BROTH #1 or #2 until done (see gluten procedure). Remove from broth and let cool. Soak in TERIYAKI SAUCE for 10 to 20 minutes. Place on oiled cookie sheet, use soy or olive oil. Spray or baste tops of gluten pieces with same oil. Bake at 350° for 20 minutes. Turn pieces over and continuing baking 10-15 minutes, until edges are crisp and well browned.

Procedure for assembling BBQ:

Cut 1 quart of onion chunks and 1 quart of green pepper chunks. Saute onions and green peppers in 2 Tbs. olive oil until about ¾ done. Add vegetables and one recipe of baked gluten to one recipe of BBQ SAUCE, 9 cups. Also add to this 2-3 c. pineapple chunks, drained. Place all of this in a baking dish. Bake at 350° until heated throughout.

YIELD: 1½ gallon

Variations: May add to mixture 6-8 cherry tomatoes, 2 Tbs. basil and/or salt to taste.

Continued on next page...

MEATLESS ENTREES

BBQ SAUCE

3½ c. pineapple juice
3½ c. tomato puree
1 c. corn syrup or ⅔ c. honey
⅓ c. lemon juice
½ c. soy sauce, unfermented

3 Tbs. oil
⅛ tsp. garlic powder
1/16 tsp. coriander
1/16 tsp. anise, ground

YIELD: 9 c.

PEPPER STEAKS

After gluten has been kneaded cut one recipe of gluten into pieces 2" x 1½" x ¼". Boil in BROTH #1 or #2 until done (see gluten procedure). Remove from broth and let cool. Soak in TERIYAKI SAUCE for 10 to 20 minutes. Dip gluten pieces in SOY SOUR CREAM or SOY MAYONNAISE. Then dip in SEASONED BREAD CRUMBS. Then place on oiled cookie sheet, using soy or olive oil. Spray or lightly baste tops of pieces with the same oil. Bake at 350° for 5-6 minutes. Turn and continue to bake another 5-6 minutes until crisp. OR, after dipping in bread crumbs, may saute in oil in fry pan until crisp. Finally, cut 1 quart onions, thickly sliced and 1 quart green peppers, thickly sliced. Saute vegetables together in 2 Tbs. soy oil. Gently fold gluten into vegetables and serve.

YIELD: 3-4 quarts

ORIENTAL PASTA

4 c. cooked whole grain spirals (see How to Cook Whole Grain Pasta)
2 Tbs. sesame oil
1½ Tbs. soy sauce, unfermented
¼ tsp. salt
¼ tsp. garlic powder
½ tsp. coriander
¼ c. finely diced red pepper OR slightly steamed carrots

¼ c. chopped scallions
½ c. rehydrated Hijiki seaweed (see note)
¼ c. frozen green peas, thawed OR ⅓ c. steamed broccoli flowers
1½ tsp. honey

Put pasta into bowl. Add remaining ingredients and stir together. Serve.
YIELD: 5 c.

Note: To rehydrate, soak ¾ c. dry Hijiki (using ¼ of a 2.75 oz. (78g) bag) in 1 c. hot water, 1½ tsp. lemon juice and ¼ c. soy sauce for 30 minutes. Drain.
YIELD: 1 c.

MUSHROOM PASTA

3 Tbs. olive oil
1 Tbs. minced garlic clove (approx. 2 large)
½ tsp. oregano
1 tsp. basil
1½ c. fresh mushrooms, whole
1½ tsp. salt
2 tsp. onion powder

½ tsp. garlic powder
½ c. chopped scallions (w/tops)
¾ c. whole or halved pitted black olives
⅓ c. chopped pimentos
4 c. cooked whole grain spirals (see How to Cook Whole Grain Pasta)

In skillet, briefly saute first four ingredients. Add next four ingredients and saute on medium heat for 15 minutes, stirring frequently. Remove from heat, put into bowl. Add remainder and mix well. Serve or chill.
YIELD: 4½ c.

SALADS, VEGETABLES, SOUPS...

TOFU "EGG" SALAD

2 c. crumbled tofu
2 c. water
2 Tbs. COUNTRY-STYLE
SEASONING
½ c. Soyagen
¾ tsp. salt

1 tsp. onion powder
½ c. soy, corn or safflower oil
1 Tbs. lemon juice
1 c. finely chopped celery
½ c. finely chopped onions
½ tsp. salt

Rinse, drain, crumble and measure tofu. Put into saucepan with next two ingredients. Stir several times and boil 20 minutes. Drain tofu, saving broth. Put into bowl and refrigerate for 20 minutes. Blend ½ cup of broth with next three ingredients on high for 5 seconds. While blender is running, slowly dribble in oil. Continue to blend for one more minute. Stop blender and stir in lemon juice for 5 seconds. When tofu is cool, add ½ cup of mayonnaise from blender along with remaining ingredients. Mix together well. Delicious as a sandwich or stuffing for tomatoes or celery.
YIELD: 2½ c.

THREE BEAN SALAD

2 c. COOKED KIDNEY
BEANS
2 c. cooked green or wax
beans
2 c. COOKED GARBANZOS
1 c. onion rings or strips
½ c. chopped or sliced black
olives

2 Tbs. chopped pimento
¼ c. lemon juice
¼ c. honey
¼ c. olive, soy, safflower,
corn or canola oil
1 Tbs. soy sauce

Put all ingredients into bowl and stir together. Cover and marinate in refrigerator for several hours or overnight. Add 1 tsp. salt if beans are salt free.
YIELD: 7 c.

GARBANZO SALAD

4 c. COOKED GARBANZOS
1 c. finely chopped celery
¾ c. finely chopped onions
¾ c. SOY MAYONNAISE
2 Tbs. lemon juice

1½ tsp. onion powder
¼ tsp. garlic powder
1½ Tbs. COUNTRY-STYLE
SEASONING

Continued on next page...

SALADS, VEGETABLES, SOUPS...

Drain garbanzos. Put into bowl and mash. Add remaining ingredients and mix together well.

YIELD: 4 c.

Note: If garbanzo are not salt free rinse well before mashing.

LENTIL SALAD

3 c. COOKED LENTILS	⅓ c. finely chopped green
¼ c. olive oil	peppers
2 Tbs. lemon juice	½ c. thinly sliced celery
1¼ tsp. salt	2 Tbs. fresh chopped parsley
2 tsp. minced garlic cloves	2 tsp. dill weed
⅓ c. finely chopped onions	½ c. chopped tomatoes

Be sure to cook lentils without salt until just tender but not mushy. Drain well and put into bowl. Blend next four ingredients on high for 5-10 seconds. Add to lentils along with remaining ingredients. Stir all together well. Chill and serve.

YIELD: 4 c.

FRENCH DRESSING

1 c. soy, corn, safflower or canola oil	¾ c. tomato puree
⅓ c. lemon juice	1 Tbs. onion powder
⅓ c. honey	½ tsp. garlic powder
1 Tbs. paprika	1½ tsp. salt

Blend all ingredients on high for 30 seconds. Chill in covered container.

YIELD: 2⅓ c.

GARLIC DRESSING

1 c. olive oil	1 tsp. salt
3 medium garlic cloves	½ c. lemon juice

Continued on next page...

Blend all ingredients on high 20-30 seconds until creamy.
YIELD: 1¼ c.

ITALIAN DRESSING

2¼ c. **soy, corn, safflower or canola oil**	1½ Tbs. **onion powder**
¾ c. **lemon juice**	1 Tbs. **basil**
1½ tsp. **salt**	2 tsp. **dried parsley**
1½ tsp. **garlic powder**	

Blend first five ingredients on high for 1-2 minutes. Pour into small bowl and stir in basil and parsley. Chill.
YIELD: 3 c.
Variation: May use ½ olive oil and ½ soy oil.

SAVORY BOUQUET

1 c. **water**	½ tsp. **garlic powder**
½ c. **sunflower seeds**	⅛ tsp. **thyme**
½ tsp. **salt**	1 tsp. **basil**
½ tsp. **onion powder**	2 Tbs. **lemon juice**

Blend all ingredients on high 1-2 minutes until creamy. A light and tasty dressing. May add a few black olives.
YIELD: 1¾ c.

THOUSAND ISLAND DRESSING

1 c. **SOY MAYONNAISE**	1 Tbs. **finely chopped onions or scallions**
⅓ c. **KETCHUP**	
2 Tbs. **finely chopped black olives**	2 tsp. **finely chopped parsley**
1 Tbs. **finely chopped green pepper**	

Put all ingredients into bowl and stir together well.

Continued on next page...

YIELD: 1⅓ c.

Variation: For a pungent dressing, substitute ENCHILADA SAUCE for KETCHUP.

——— QUICK THOUSAND ISLAND DRESSING ———

1 c. SOY MAYONNAISE
⅓ c. TOMATO SAUCE

2 Tbs. finely chopped black olives

Mix all ingredients together in bowl. Chill.
YIELD: 1⅓ c.

——— OLIVE DRESSING ———
(with SOY BASE)

½ c. water
½ c. SOY BASE
¾ tsp. salt
1½ tsp. onion powder

½ c. soy, corn, safflower or canola oil
½ c. pitted black olives
1½ Tbs. lemon juice

Blend first four ingredients on high for 30 seconds. While blender is running, slowly dribble in oil. Whiz for one full minute after adding oil. Stop blender and add olives. Blend for 5 seconds. Stop blender and stir in lemon juice for 5-10 seconds.
YIELD: 2 c.

Variation: To make into dip, increase oil to ¾ c.

——— OLIVE DRESSING ———
(with Soyagen)

1 c. water
½ c. Soyagen
½ tsp. salt
1 tsp. onion powder

¼ c. soy, corn, safflower or canola oil
½ c. pitted black olives
4 tsp. lemon juice

Continued on next page...

Blend first four ingredients on high for 10-15 seconds. While blender is running, slowly dribble in oil. Blend for one full minute after adding oil. Stop blender and add olives. Blend for 5 seconds. Stop blender and stir in lemon juice for 5-10 seconds.

YIELD: 2¼ c.

Variation: To make into dip, increase oil to ½ c.

CUCUMBER DRESSING

¼ c. water
½ c. SOY BASE
1 tsp. salt
1½ tsp. onion powder

¼ c. soy, corn, safflower or canola oil
½ c. chopped cucumbers
1½ Tbs. lemon juice

Blend first four ingredients on high for 30 seconds. While blender is running, slowly dribble in oil. Blend for one full minute after adding oil. Stop blender and put in cucumbers. Blend for 3 seconds. Stop blender and stir in lemon juice for 5-10 seconds.

YIELD: 1½ c.

Variation: To make into dip, increase oil to ½ c.

CUCUMBER DRESSING (with Soyagen)

1 c. water
½ c. Soyagen
¾ tsp. salt
1 tsp. onion powder

¼ c. soy, corn, safflower or canola oil
½ c. chopped cucumbers
4 tsp. lemon juice

Blend first four ingredients on high for 10-15 seconds. While blender is running, slowly dribble in oil. Blend one full minute after adding oil. Stop blender and put in cucumbers. Blend for 3 seconds. Stop blender and stir in lemon juice for 5-10 seconds. Chill.

YIELD: 2¼ c.

Variation: To make into dip, increase oil to ½ c.

SALADS, VEGETABLES, SOUPS...

SAUCE ROGUE
(Dressing from Country Life, Paris)

⅔ c. olive oil
⅔ c. soy oil
¾ c. fresh chopped tomatoes
1½ Tbs. yeast flakes

2 tsp. salt
1-2 garlic cloves
½ tsp. marjoram

Blend all ingredients on high for 1-2 minutes until creamy.
YIELD: 1¾ c.

EMULTION
(Dressing from Country Life, Paris)

1 c. sesame oil
⅓ c. olive oil
3 medium garlic cloves
2 tsp. soy sauce
3 Tbs. yeast flakes
1 tsp. marjoram

1 tsp. savory
8 walnuts
1 Tbs. lemon juice
¼ c. SOY MILK
¾ tsp. salt, optional

Blend all ingredients on high 1-2 minutes until creamy.
YIELD: 1¾ c.

SOY MAYONNAISE #1
(with SOY MILK)

1 c. SOY MILK
½ tsp. salt
½ tsp. onion powder

1 c. soy, corn, safflower or
canola oil
2 Tbs. lemon juice

Blend first three ingredients on high 5-10 seconds. Slowly dribble in oil, blending for an additional full minute after all of oil has been added. Stop blender and stir in lemon juice. Put into covered container and chill.
YIELD: 2 c.

SOY MAYONNAISE #2
(with SOY BASE)

½ c. water
½ c. SOY BASE
1 tsp. salt

1½ tsp. onion powder
¾ c. soy, corn or safflower oil
1½ Tbs. lemon juice

Blend first four ingredients on high for 30 seconds. While blender is running, slowly dribble in oil. Continue to blend for one full minute after oil is added. Stop blender and stir in lemon juice for 5-10 seconds.
YIELD: 1¾ c.
Note: When using fresh-made, hot SOY BASE, only ½ c. oil is needed.
YIELD: 1½ c.

SOY MAYONNAISE #3
(with Soyagen)

1 c. water
½ c. Soyagen
¾ tsp. salt
1 tsp. onion powder

½ c. soy, corn, safflower or
canola oil
4 tsp. lemon juice

Blend first four ingredients on high for 10-15 seconds. While blender is running, slowly dribble in oil. Continue to blend for one full minute after oil is added. Stop blender and stir in lemon juice for 5-10 seconds.
YIELD: 2 c.

TAHINI MAYONNAISE

1 c. water
1 c. tahini
1½ tsp. onion powder

½ tsp. garlic powder
1 tsp. salt
¼ c. lemon juice

Blend all ingredients on high for 30 seconds until creamy.
YIELD: 2¼ c.
Variation: For dressing, use ¾ c. tahini.
YIELD: 2 c.

SALADS, VEGETABLES, SOUPS...

CASHEW MAYONNAISE

1 c. water
½ c. cashew pieces
pinch of garlic powder

¾ tsp. salt
¾ tsp. onion powder
2 Tbs. lemon juice

Blend all ingredients, except lemon juice, on high 1-2 minutes until creamy. Pour into sauce pan and cook over medium-high stirring constantly until thickened (approx. 5 minutes). Remove from heat and stir in lemon juice. Put into covered container and chill.
YIELD: 1 c.

TOFU MAYONNAISE

1 c. crumbled tofu
¼ c. water
½ tsp. salt
1½ tsp. onion powder

⅛ tsp. garlic powder
¼ c. soy, safflower, corn or
    canola oil
1 tsp. lemon

Rinse, drain, crumble and measure tofu. Put into blender and add remaining ingredients. Blend on high for one minute until creamy. Keep refrigerated. Will last 3-4 days.
YIELD: 1¼ c.

AIOLI or GARLIC MAYONNAISE #1
(with SOY MILK)

Very popular in France where it is sometimes known as "Beurre de Provence".

1 c. SOY MILK
½ tsp. salt
½ tsp. onion powder
2 medium garlic cloves

½ c. soy, corn, safflower or
    canola oil
¼ c. olive oil
2 Tbs. lemon juice

Blend first three ingredients on high 5-10 seconds. Slowly dribble in oil, blending for an additional full minute after all of oil has been added. Stop blender and stir in lemon juice. Put into covered container and chill.
YIELD: 2 c.

SALADS, VEGETABLES, SOUPS...

AIOLI or GARLIC MAYONNAISE #2

1 c. water
½ c. Soyagen
¾ tsp. salt

2 medium garlic cloves
½ c. olive oil
4 tsp. lemon juice

Blend first four ingredients on high for 30 seconds. While blender is running, slowly dribble in oil. Blend for one full minute after adding oil. Stop blender and stir in lemon juice for 10-15 seconds. Delicious on pizza or served with raw or steamed vegetables.

YIELD: 1¾ c.

Variation: May use SOY BASE in place of Soyagen. Decrease water to ½ c. and increase salt to 1 tsp.

YIELD: 2 c.

SOY SOUR CREAM

Follow recipe for SOY MAYONNAISE increasing lemon juice to 2-2½ Tbs. Stir in 1 Tbs. dried or 2 Tbs. fresh chives. Delicious on baked potatoes, crackers or as a dip for raw vegetables.

SUNFLOWER SOUR CREAM

1¼ c. water
1 c. sunflower seeds
1 tsp. salt

1 tsp. onion powder
½ tsp. garlic powder
⅓ c. lemon juice

Blend all ingredients on high 2-3 minutes until creamy.

YIELD: 2 c.

Variation: To use as a dressing follow recipe increasing water to 1⅔ c., onion powder to 1½ tsp. and decreasing lemon juice to 3 Tbs.

YIELD: 2½ c.

SOY MARGARINE #1

¾ c. water
½ c. Soyagen
1 tsp. salt

2 tsp. liquid lecithin
2 tsp. tahini
1 c. soy, corn or safflower oil

Continued on next page...

Blend first five ingredients on high for 20-30 seconds until creamy. While blender is running, slowly dribble in oil. Continue to blend for one more minute. Chill in covered container.

YIELD: 1½ c.

Note: For a firm margarine, use ½ c. soy oil and ½ c. coconut oil.

SOY MARGARINE #2

¾ c. water
1 c. SOY BASE
1 tsp. salt
¾ tsp. onion powder

¼ c. chopped raw or cooked carrots
1¼ c. soy, safflower, corn or canola oil

Blend first five ingredients on high for 1-2 minutes until creamy. While blender is running, slowly dribble in oil. Continue to blend for one minute. Chill in covered container.

YIELD: 3 c.

TASTY CORN "MARGARINE" SPREAD

½ c. coconut or cashew pieces
½ c. hot water
½ tsp. salt

¼ tsp. maple flavoring (optional)
1 c. FRESHLY COOKED CORNMEAL

Blend first four ingredients on high for 30 seconds until creamy. Stop blender and add cornmeal. Blend on high again until smooth. Pour into container and chill.

YIELD: 1⅔ c.

GOLDEN GARLIC MUSTARD

¾ c. lemon juice
¼ c. soy flour
½ tsp. salt
1½ tsp. turmeric or paprika

2 Tbs. chopped garlic cloves
¼ c. soy, corn or safflower oil

Continued on next page...

Blend first four ingredients on high for 15-20 seconds until creamy. Pour into saucepan and cook over medium heat stirring constantly until thickened. Cool. Return to blender and add garlic. Whiz on high, slowly dribbling in oil. Continue to blend for one more minute. Put into container. Cover & chill.

YIELD: 1 c. (Veg-A-Weigh Recipe)

KETCHUP

1⅓ c. tomato paste (1 - 12 oz. can)	2 Tbs. olive oil
½ c. tomato puree	¼ tsp. oregano
2-4 Tbs. honey	2 tsp. onion powder
2 Tbs. lemon juice	¼ tsp. garlic powder
	1 tsp. salt

Put all ingredients into bowl and stir together well. Keep refrigerated.

YIELD: 2½ c.

Variation: For CHILI KETCHUP stir in 1 Tbs. CHILI SEASONING.

PIMENTO CHEESE SAUCE

1 c. water	1¼ tsp. salt
¾ c. cashew pieces or tahini	2 tsp. onion powder
2 Tbs. sesame seeds or 1 Tbs. tahini (omit when using tahini)	¼ tsp. garlic powder
	½ c. pimentos
3 Tbs. yeast flakes	2 Tbs. lemon juice
	⅛ tsp. dill seed, optional

Blend all ingredients on high 1-2 minutes until creamy. Very versatile cheese sauce. Use as dressing for salad or steamed vegetables, with pasta, potatoes or in lasagne.

YIELD: 2¼ c.

Variation: In place of ¾ c. cashews, use 6 Tbs. cashews and 6 Tbs. tahini. Omit sesame seeds. Has a mild cheesy flavor.

Note: When using cashews, may pour into saucepan and cook over medium-high, stirring constantly until thickened.

SALADS, VEGETABLES, SOUPS...

———————— PIMENTO CHEESE BRICK ————————

1½ c. water
5 Tbs. agar flakes (see
    (Potpourri)
¾ c. cashew pieces or tahini
2 Tbs. sesame seeds or 1 Tbs.
    tahini (omit when using
    tahini)

1¼ tsp. salt
2 tsp. onion powder
¼ tsp. garlic powder
¼ c. yeast flakes
½ c. pimentos
2½ Tbs. lemon juice

Put first two ingredients into small saucepan and bring to boil. Reduce heat to medium and simmer for 5 minutes, stirring frequently. Place remaining ingredients in blender. Add agar mixture when cooked. Blend all ingredients on high 1-2 minutes until creamy, stopping blender once or twice to stir contents. Pour into mold and chill overnight.

YIELD: 2½ c.

Variations: To make different flavors, fold in one of the following before pouring cheese into mold.
1. Olive – ¾ c. finely chopped olives
2. Toasted Sesame – 2 Tbs. TOASTED SESAME SEEDS
3. Caraway – 1½ Tbs. caraway seeds
4. Dill – 2 Tbs. dill weed
5. Onion-Dill – 1 Tbs. + 2 tsp. dehydrated onion flakes and 2¼ tsp. dill seed or dill weed

———————————— LESSARELLA CHEEZ ————————————

2 c. water
3 Tbs. lemon juice
½ c. yeast flakes
⅓ c. quick oats

¼ c. arrowroot or cornstarch
1 Tbs. onion powder
¼ c. tahini
1½ tsp. salt

Blend all ingredients on high for one minute. Pour into saucepan and cook on medium, stirring constantly until thickened. Put into loaf pan or other mold. Chill overnight. Remove from mold and slice. Delicious on crackers, pizza or in sandwiches.

May sprinkle on herbs and melt under broiler.

YIELD: 2¾ c. or 1 medium loaf pan.

Variation: For pizza or fondue, use half the amount of arrowroot.

SALADS, VEGETABLES, SOUPS...

GARBANZO CHEESE

1 c. **dry garbanzos**	1 tsp. **dill seed or ½ tsp.**
½ c. **Brazil nuts, cashews,**	**caraway or celery seed**
filberts or almonds	⅓ c. **yeast flakes**
2 tsp. **onion powder**	½ c. **pimentos**
1¾ tsp. **salt**	1 c. **water**
½ tsp. **garlic powder**	¼ c. **lemon juice**

Soak garbanzos in cold water for 24 hours. After soaking, rinse and drain. Place in bowl uncovered at room temperature and let sprout for 2 days. Rinse daily in colander with cool water. After 2 days, measure 2 c. of sprouted garbanzos and put in blender. Add remaining ingredients and whiz on high 1-3 minutes until smooth. Pour into saucepan and cook over medium heat for 20 minutes stirring constantly. Remove from heat and pack into jar, loaf pan or mold that has been rinsed in cold water. Chill for several hours or overnight. Turn out of mold and slice.

YIELD: 3 c.

Note: In warm weather, refrigerate garbanzos while soaking and rinse twice a day.

CHEESE FONDUE

This traditional Swiss dish is usually made from melted cheese. But did you know you can enjoy a cheese fondue without cheese? Make LEZZERELLA CHEESE with ½ the arrowroot; or prepare PIMENTO CHEESE with cashews, cooking over medium-high while stirring constantly until thickened. Rub inside the fondue dish with garlic clove. Put thickened sauce into pot and keep warm. Dip CROUTONS or cubes of crusty French Bread on fondue forks into cheese and enjoy. Served with fresh fruit this makes a delightful summer meal.

TOFU COTTAGE CHEESE

4 c. **mashed tofu**	½ tsp. **garlic powder**
1½ tsp. **salt**	¾ c. **SOY MAYONNAISE**
2¼ tsp. **onion powder**	2 Tbs. **dried parsley or chives**

Rinse, drain and mash tofu. Measure 4 c. and put into bowl. Add remaining ingredients and mix together well. Chill.

YIELD: 4 c.

SALADS, VEGETABLES, SOUPS...

GUACAMOLE

2 c. mashed avocado (approx.
2 medium)
1 tsp. garlic powder
1½ tsp. onion powder

1 tsp. salt
1½ Tbs. lemon juice
¾ c. finely chopped tomatoes

Scoop out avocadoes into bowl and mash well. Add remaining ingredients and mix together. Chill. Makes a delicious dip for raw vegetables or a spread on bread.

YIELD: 2¾ c.

HUMMUS
(A Middle Eastern Chickpea Puree)

2 c. COOKED GARBANZOS
drained
4-6 Tbs. lemon juice
1⅛ tsp. salt
½ c. tahini

⅓-½ c. garbanzo juice or water
1¼ tsp. onion powder
4 garlic cloves OR 1 tsp.
garlic powder

Blend all ingredients on high 1-2 minutes until creamy. A delicious spread or dip.

YIELD: 2½ c.

Note: For a dressing, double the water.

BABA GANNOUJ
(A Middle Eastern Eggplant/Tahini Puree)

1 c. eggplant (about 1 pound)
1 minced garlic clove
2 Tbs. fresh lemon juice
¼ c. tahini

1 Tbs. olive oil
3 Tbs. finely chopped parsley
¾ tsp. salt

Rinse eggplant and place on cookie sheet whole. Bake at 350° until eggplant collapses and is softened throughout, about 25 minutes. Remove from heat and let cool. Scrape away flesh from skin and put into blender or food processor (about 1 c.) Add remaining ingredients and blend on high until pureed. Serve hot or cold.

YIELD: 1⅓-1½ c. (depending on size of eggplant).

SALADS, VEGETABLES, SOUPS...

OLIVE CAVIAR

1½ c. finely chopped black
    olives (about 3 c. whole)
2 Tbs. olive oil
2 Tbs. minced garlic cloves
1 tsp. basil

½ tsp. thyme
¾ tsp. savory (crush after
    measuring)
¾ tsp. salt
1½ tsp. lemon juice

Chop olives in food processor or blender and put into bowl. In small skillet, saute next five ingredients several minutes, stirring often. Add to olives along with remaining ingredients and mix together well. Cover and refrigerate overnight. Delicious on crackers or stuffed into celery.

YIELD: 1½ c.

FRENCH PÂTÉ

½# of a loaf of whole grain
    bread (do not use fruit/
    nut varieties)
⅓ c. water
2 Tbs. olive oil
1 bay leaf
1½ tsp. thyme
2 c. finely chopped onions

¼ tsp. marjoram
1 tsp. ITALIAN SEASONING
1½ tsp. basil
1½ Tbs. yeast flakes
¾ tsp. salt
1 tsp. minced garlic clove
¼ c. non-dairy margarine
    (see note)

Make loaf into crumbs and put into bowl. (See how to make WHOLE GRAIN BREAD CRUMBS.) Add water and mix. Set aside. In large skillet, briefly saute next three ingredients. Put in onions. Cover and cook over medium heat until soft (approx. 20 minutes). When onions are done, remove bay leaf and add next six ingredients along with bread crumbs. Stir. Cover and cook over low heat for 15 minutes. In small saucepan, slowly melt margarine. Put pate into bowl and add melted margarine. Mix well. Cover and chill. Delicious on crackers.

YIELD: 3 c.

Note: Be sure to use a hardened non-dairy margarine such as Willow Run or Shedd's. May make our MARGARINE #1 with ½ coconut oil.

SALADS, VEGETABLES, SOUPS...

BAKED GARLIC

Garlic prepared in this way has a mild and delightful flavor.

1 head or bulb of garlic	¼ tsp. thyme
1 tsp. olive oil	shake of salt

Remove outer casing from garlic head. Leave whole or separate cloves. Cut one square of aluminum foil large enough to completely enclose bulb. Place garlic in center of foil. Dribble on oil and sprinkle with thyme and salt. Seal in foil. Leave space around garlic to expand. Bake at 325° for one hour. Serve with CROUTONS, bread or CRUDITES. Squeeze cloves onto bread for a satisfying butter substitute, or just peel and eat.

GOMASIO

1 c. unhulled sesame seeds	½ tsp. salt

In dry skillet, toast sesame seeds on medium-high stirring constantly until slightly browned and beginning to crackle (about 5 minutes). Remove from heat; add salt and mix. Blend on high for 5 seconds. Stop blender and stir. Blend 5 more seconds. (Should NOT be ground fine.) Pour into container and stir once more. An excellent seasoning on salads, rice or vegetables as well as in entrees or patties.
YIELD: 1½ c.

SESAME SPRINKLE
(Parmesan-like Topping)

1 c. unhulled sesame seeds	½ tsp. garlic powder
2 tsp. salt	2 Tbs. COUNTRY-STYLE
1 c. yeast flakes	SEASONING
2 tsp. onion powder	2 Tbs. lemon juice

In dry skillet, toast sesame seeds on medium-high stirring constantly until slightly browned and beginning to crackle (about 5 minutes). Remove from heat and blend on high until finely ground. Pour into bowl and add remaining ingredients. Mix together well with hands. Keep refrigerated. Delicious sprinkled on salads, vegetables or spaghetti.
YIELD: 2 c.

SALADS, VEGETABLES, SOUPS...

SEASONED CROUTONS #1

Brush lightly one side of sliced whole grain bread with vegetable oil of your choice. (Olive is best). Sprinkle oiled side of bread with onion powder, garlic powder, salt, basil and/or oregano to taste. (May use your choice of herbs). Cut bread into 1" cubes and place on cookie sheet. Dry in 250° oven for about one hour. Delicious in soups or salads.

SEASONED CROUTONS #2

8 c. 1" whole grain bread cubes	1 Tbs. garlic powder
⅓ c. warm water	1½ tsp. oregano
2 Tbs. olive oil	1 Tbs. basil
1 Tbs. onion powder	½ tsp. salt

Lay bread cubes on cookie sheet and dry in 250° oven for about 1-1½ hours. Place in bowl. Put remaining ingredients into small bowl and whisk together well. Pour over croutons and mix together.
YIELD: 7 c.

CRUDITÉS
(cut-up vegetables)

The idea of crudités came from Provence in southern France. Its warm climate and sunshine produces an abundance of vegetables. The American concept of crudités is commonly called a raw vegetable platter. But in its most artistic form it goes much beyond the usual carrot and celery sticks and cherry tomatoes.

With air shipments and hothouse culture there is an ever-expanding array of produce from which to select. Many wonderful varieties are now available regardless of the season. So break out of the narrow confines of the familiar and traditional and delve into the enjoyment of the unusual: kohlrabi, sunchokes, fennel, or chinese cabbage to name but a few. Select the freshest, most perfect vegetables possible. Be sure to store properly without delay to insure preservation of the best appearance.

In preparing vegetables for display, the object is to make something that is not too large to be eaten in one or two bites nor too small to be handled gracefully. Some vegetables can be left whole, others cut up. You can be simple or elaborate. There are several excellent books available on the art

Continued on next page...

SALADS, VEGETABLES, SOUPS...

of creating beautiful curls, crisps and feathers. Slant cutting of carrots, celery or zucchini offer a nice effect without much effort. For variety, traditional pepper strips can be transformed into chunks. Sugar snap peas, tender green beans and asparagus are wonderful left whole. Remember, the best displays are simple.

In the arrangement of the vegetables, be sure to contrast color and shapes. Beside the usual platter, baskets provide a warm medium for display. It is also intriguing to put one vegetable inside another; for instance, green beans or asparagus inside a hollowed out pumpkin or cabbage. Be creative and surprise yourself at what you can do.

There are several vegetables whose color and digestibility are enhanced by blanching, which involves a quick immersion into rapidly boiling water. This maximizes flavor and color and makes them tender yet crispy. Blanch no longer than six hours before use. Immerse immediately into ice cold water. Drain well, cover with paper towels. Wrap in plastic and refrigerate until ready to use.

Blanching times:
cauliflower – 5-6 minutes
broccoli – 3 minutes
brussel sprouts – 8 minutes
asparagus – 3-5 minutes, depending on thickness of stalk
green beans – 2-4 minutes
carrots – 3 minutes
snowpeas – 30 seconds

Serve your credités with OLIVE or CUCUMBER DRESSING, SOUR CREAM, HUMMUS, or slices of PIMENTO CHEESE BRICK.

Bon Appétit

TOFU TOMATO STARS

Cut fresh, ripe tomatoes into quarters or 6ths, three-fourths of the way through lengthwise. Open tomato star and fill with TOFU COTTAGE CHEESE. Sprinkle with paprika and garnish with a fresh parsley sprig or olive. A delicious summer salad.

TOMATO BASKETS

Slice firm, ripe tomatoes across top about ½ inch below stem. Scoop out pulp into a bowl. Add GARBANZO SALAD and stir together well. Stuff tomato with mixture, slightly mounding at top. Garnish with a sprig of fresh parsley.

SALADS, VEGETABLES, SOUPS...

BAKED TOMATOES A LA PROVENCALE

8 medium tomatoes (do not use plum tomatoes)
2-4 tsp. GROUND HERBES DE PROVENCE

½ c. AIOLI
8 pitted black olives

Slice off top of tomatoes ½ inch below stem. Place cut side up in LECITHIN-OILED 8" x 8" baking dish. Lightly salt and sprinkle with herbs to taste. (grind HERBES DE PROVENCE in seed mill or blender). Add 1 Tbs. AIOLI to each tomato. Top with olives. Bake at 350° for one hour or until tomatoes are tender.
YIELD: 8 baked tomatoes

STEWED TOMATOES

1 minced garlic clove
¼ c. finely chopped onions
1 Tbs. olive oil
6 c. canned tomatoes in puree

1 tsp. basil
¼ tsp. thyme
⅛ tsp. marjoram
1 Tbs. dried parsley

Saute first three ingredients in pot until onions are clear. Measure tomatoes with puree. Crush with hands and pour into pot. Add remaining ingredients, cover and simmer for 30 minutes.
YIELD: 5½ c.

TOMATOES & ZUCCHINI

1 recipe STEWED TOMATOES

3 c. chopped zucchini, ¾"

Prepare 1 recipe of STEWED TOMATO. Before simmering, add zucchini. Simmer together for 30 minutes. Delicious served over pasta.
YIELD: 6 c.

SALADS, VEGETABLES, SOUPS...

ZUCCHINI FILLETS

Wash zucchini and remove stems. Cut into ½" slices lengthwise. Dip into BREADING MEAL and place on LECITHIN-OILED cookie sheet. May lightly salt. Bake at 350° for 15 minutes on each side.

This is an excellent way to use overgrown zucchini. May also remove stems and cut into ½" circles. Bread and bake same as above. Delicious in a sandwich with SOY MAYONNAISE and a slice of tomato.

BAKED EGGPLANT

14 eggplant slices (approx. 1 large)	**½ c. yeast flakes**
1 c. SOY MAYONNAISE	**½ c. wheat germ or unrefined cornmeal**
½ c. tomato paste	

Cut eggplant into ½" slices. To make coating, mix together mayonnaise and tomato paste in small bowl. Combine last two ingredients in another small bowl to make breading meal. Coat one side of eggplant slice. Dip into breading. Repeat with other side of slice. Place on a cookie sheet. Follow same procedure with remaining slices. Bakes at 350° for 10 minutes. Flip over and bake an additional 10 minutes.

YIELD: 14 slices

LEEKS AU GRATIN

6 c. chopped fresh leeks   **3 c. PIMENTO CHEESE SAUCE**

Cut roots off leeks and wash well in cold water. Drain chop into one inch pieces. Steam for 15 minutes and put into bowl. Add PIMENTO CHEESE and mix together. Put into LECITHIN-OILED 8" x 8" baking dish. Bake at 350° for 30 minutes. Delicious.

YIELD: 7 c.

SALADS, VEGETABLES, SOUPS...

ONION PIE

1-2 minced garlic cloves	¼ tsp. garlic powder
1¼ tsp. thyme	1 tsp. salt
1 Tbs. olive oil	1¼ c. water #2
4 c. finely sliced onions	1½ tsp. dried parsley
¼ tsp. salt	2 Tbs. cornstarch
½ c. cashew pieces	¾ recipe of FLAKY WHEAT-OAT
¾ c. water #1	PIE CRUST
2 Tbs. onion powder	

In skillet, briefly saute first three ingredients together. Add onions and salt and simmer 40 minutes, until well-cooked but not browned. As onions are cooking, blend next five ingredients on high 1-2 minutes until creamy. Stop blender and add water #2, dried parsley and cornstarch. Blend on high for 3-5 seconds. Pour into bowl and add cooked onions and juice. Mix together well.

Make pie dough. (See FLAKY WHEAT-OAT PIE CRUST for specific directions.) Line 10" quiche dish or 10" pie pan. Top crust with onion mixture. Bake at 350° for 30 minutes.

YIELD: 4 c. or 1 - 10" pie

Variation: May add whole or chopped black olives before baking.

CREAMED CUCUMBERS

8 c. very thinly sliced peeled cucumbers (about 6-7" cucumbers)	2 c. SOY MAYONNAISE or SOY SOUR CREAM
2 Tbs. salt	½ c. finely chopped onions

Put cucumber slices into bowl and sprinkle with salt. Mix together well. Cover bowl with plastic wrap and refrigerate 6-7 hours (overnight is best). Pour cucumbers into colander and rinse thoroughly under cold water, squeezing to remove all salt. Let stand about 10 more minutes. Put into another bowl and add remaining ingredients. Mix and serve. Absolutely scrumptious!

YIELD: 4 c.

SALADS, VEGETABLES, SOUPS...

——— CREAMED POTATOES & CUCUMBERS ———

2 lbs. potatoes (6 c.)   1 tsp. salt
3 c. CREAMED CUCUMBERS

Clean potatoes and cut into 2" chunks with skins. Put into pot and cook in 2" of water until tender (about 20 minutes). Pour off water and mash. Put potatoes into a bowl and add remaining ingredients. Mix and serve.
YIELD: 9 c.

——————— MASHED POTATOES ———————

Follow recipe for EARLY MORNING POTATO PANCAKES. Do not form into patties. Mash and serve.

——————— SOUR CREAM POTATOES ———————

2 lbs. potatoes (6 c.)   1 tsp. garlic powder
2 c. SOY SOUR CREAM or   1 tsp. salt
      MAYONNAISE   1 Tbs. onion powder

Clean potatoes leaving on skin. Boil until tender. Drain and cut into ¾" chunks. Put into bowl. Add remaining ingredients and stir together. Serve immediately or bake at 350° for 30 minutes in LECITHIN-OILED 8" x 8" baking dish.
YIELD: 7½ c.
Variations: May add black olives, parsley or chives.

——————— BAKED SWEET POTATOES ———————

8 c. raw, sliced sweet   2 c. GRANOLA of your choice
      potatoes, ¼"   2 c. coconut, walnuts or
3 c. unsweetened pineapple   pecans
      juice
½ tsp. salt

Continued on next page...

Wash sweet potatoes, leaving on skins. Cut off ends and slice. Steam for 15 minutes. Put into LECITHIN-OILED 9" x 13" baking dish. Add salt to pineapple juice and pour over potatoes. Blend half of granola and coconut together on high until finely ground, stopping blender once or twice to stir contents. Put into bowl. Repeat procedure with remainder. Mix well. Crumble evenly over potatoes. Cover and bake at 350° for 30 minutes.
YIELD: 9" x 13" baking dish

SAVORY STEAMED KALE

½ lb. fresh kale	½ c. chopped onions
2 lg. minced garlic cloves	⅓ c. water
1 Tbs. olive oil	salt to taste

Wash kale well. If leaves are small, do not chop. If leaves are larger, remove the most coarse part of stem and stack 6-8 leaves on top of one another. Cut crosswise into 1" strips. In saucepan, briefly saute garlic in olive oil on medium. Add onions and saute for 4-5 minutes until clear. Add water and kale and turn heat to medium-high. Cover and steam until tender (about 20 mintes). Larger leaves need to be cooked longer, up to 60 minutes. Add salt to taste.
YIELD: 2 c.
Note: May use collards, turnips or greens of your choice in place of kale.

HARVARD BEETS

1 c. beet juice	½ tsp. grated lemon rind
2 Tbs. cornstarch	2 Tbs. honey
¼ tsp. salt	4 c. cooked, drained beets
2 Tbs. lemon juice	(sliced or diced)

In small bowl, whisk together first three ingredients. Pour into saucepan and cook on medium-high stirring constantly until thickened. Remove from heat and stir in next three ingredients. Add beets and mix carefully. Colorful served with corn and green salad.
YIELD: 4 c.

SALADS, VEGETABLES, SOUPS...

MEDITERRANEAN BEETS

1 c. minced garlic clove
1½ tsp. basil
2 Tbs. olive oil
½ c. chopped onions
3 c. cooked drained beets,
sliced, salt free

¼ c. beet juice
2 Tbs. lemon juice
¾ tsp. salt
½ c. pitted black olives, whole

In skillet, saute first four ingredients 3-5 minutes. Stirring often add remaining ingredients. Stir together carefully and cook for several more minutes. Remove from heat. Serve hot or cold.

YIELD: 3½ c.

CREAM OF TOMATO SOUP

2 c. SOY or NUT MILK (use
cashews, omit vanilla)
2 tsp. onion powder
¼ tsp. garlic powder
¾-1 tsp. salt
⅛ tsp. oregano (optional)
¼ tsp. basil

1 Tbs. honey
1 Tbs. cornstarch (omit when
using cashew milk)
3 c. whole canned tomatoes in
juice
1 c. tomato puree

Blend first 8 ingredients on high for 5-10 seconds. Pour into saucepan. Blend canned tomatoes on high for 3 seconds until smooth. Add to saucepan. Add puree and bring to boil, stirring constantly. Cook until thickened (about 15 minutes). May serve with CROUTONS.

YIELD: 6 c.

Note: If using tomatoes canned in puree, omit tomato puree and use 4 c. canned tomatoes.

Variation: May add cooked rice or cooked pasta to desired consistency.

SALADS, VEGETABLES, SOUPS...

SUPPER TOMATO SOUP

6 c. tomato juice (1 - 46 oz. can)
1 bay leaf
¼ tsp. thyme
¼ tsp. celery seed
¼ tsp. garlic powder
1½ tsp. onion powder
½ tsp. salt
1 Tbs. dried parsley
1-2 Tbs. honey
1 Tbs. oil (optional)

Put all ingredients into saucepan and stir together. Bring to boil; reduce heat and simmer several minutes. A light evening meal served with croutons or crackers.
YIELD: 5 c.

GAZPACHO SOUP
(Cold Spanish Soup)

4 c. tomato juice
¼ c. lemon juice
2 tsp. salt
2 medium garlic cloves
¼ c. olive oil
2 c. fresh chopped tomatoes
1 c. chopped green peppers
1 c. chopped cucumber
¼ c. fresh chopped parsley
1 c. chopped celery
½ c. chopped onions
2 Tbs. fresh chopped chives (may use scallion tops)

Blend first five ingredients on high for 20-30 seconds until creamy. Pour into bowl and add remaining ingredients. Mix together gently. Cover and chill. Serve. A refreshing soup for hot weather.
YIELD: 8 c.

POTTAGE DU FROMAGE
(Cheesy Broccoli Soup)

3½ c. water
1 c. cashew pieces
2½ tsp. salt
6 Tbs. yeast flakes
2 tsp. onion powder
¼ tsp. garlic powder
½ tsp. dill weed OR ¼ tsp. dill seed
¼ c. pimentos
3-4 c. chopped broccoli (fresh is best)

Continued on next page...

SALADS, VEGETABLES, SOUPS...

Blend on high half the water with remaining ingredients except broccoli 1-2 minutes until creamy. Pour into saucepan and add rest of water and broccoli. If using fresh broccoli it should be lightly steamed before adding to soup. Cook over medium-high heat stirring constantly until slightly thickened and broccoli is tender. Delicious served with garlic bread.

YIELD: 7 c.

Variations: May use cauliflower or asparagus in place of broccoli.

FRENCH ONION SOUP

5 c. thinly sliced onions	½ c. soy sauce
1 Tbs. olive oil	2 Tbs. onion powder
8 c. water	
3 Tbs. COUNTRY-STYLE SEASONING	

In pot, saute onions in olive oil until lightly browned. In small bowl whisk together COUNTRY-STYLE SEASONING with ½ c. of water measurement. Add rest of water and remaining ingredients to pot and bring to boil. Reduce heat and simmer until onions are cooked. Served with SOY SOUR CREAM and CROUTONS.

YIELD: 10 c.

LIMA BEAN CHOWDER

3 c. water	1½ tsp. salt
1½ c. chopped onions	1½ tsp. onion powder
3 c. cubed potatoes, ¾"	1½ tsp. garlic powder
2 c. frozen kernel corn	1 tsp. dill weed
½ c. frozen or fresh fordhook limas	1-1½ c. SOY MAYONNAISE

In pot, bring to boil first five ingredients. Reduce heat to medium and cook for 10 minutes. Add four seasonings and continue to cook until vegetables are tender (approx. 10 minutes more) stir in SOY MAYONNAISE and cook for several more minutes. Serve.

YIELD: 6 c.

SALADS, VEGETABLES, SOUPS...

GARBANZO NOODLE SOUP

1 minced garlic clove
1½ tsp. olive oil
½ c. chopped onions
3 c. water
3 Tbs. COUNTRY-STYLE
SEASONING

1½ c. dry whole grain pasta
1½ c. COOKED, DRAINED
GARBANZOS
1 Tbs. dried parsley or 2 Tbs.
finely chopped fresh
parsley

In pot, lightly saute garlic in olive oil. Add onions and cook until soft. Put in next three ingredients and bring to boil. Reduce heat to medium and cook until noodles are al dente. Add last two ingredients. Heat briefly and serve. If beans are salt free add ⅛ tsp. of salt.
YIELD: 5½ c.

SIMPLE SPLIT PEA SOUP

8 c. water
2 c. dry split peas
2 Tbs. olive oil
2 c. chopped onions
2 c. chopped celery and/or
carrots

2 bay leaves
1½ Tbs. onion powder
1 tsp. garlic powder
2 tsp. salt

Put first two ingredients into pot. Bring to boil, reduce heat, cover and simmer for one half hour. Add remaining ingredients and simmer covered for one hour. Remove cover and simmer for 30 more minutes. Stir occasionally.
YIELD: 9½ c.

HEARTY LENTIL SOUP

2 minced garlic cloves
2-4 Tbs. olive oil
10 c. water
2½ c. dry lentils
2 c. chopped onions
1 c. chopped celery
2 c. diced carrots
3 Tbs. tomato paste

2 bay leaves
2½ tsp. salt
¼ tsp. celery seed
¾ tsp. oregano
¼ tsp. savory
2 Tbs. lemon juice
½ c. finely chopped parsley

Continued on next page...

In small skillet, briefly saute garlic in olive oil. Set aside. In pot, bring lentils and water to boil. Reduce heat to medium. Cover and simmer for 20 minutes until lentils are half cooked. Then add next nine ingredients. Simmer all together covered for 30 more minutes. Add lemon juice and parsley just before serving.

YIELD: 10 c.

NAVY BEAN SOUP

2 Tbs. olive oil	2 c. frozen chopped kale or
2 medium minced garlic cloves	collards (partially thawed)
1 c. chopped onions	1¾ tsp. salt
5 c. water	¼ tsp. cumin
2 c. cubed potatoes ½"	2 Tbs. yeast flakes
	3 c. COOKED NAVY BEANS

In pot, briefly saute garlic in olive oil. Add onions and continue to saute until clear. Put in next six ingredients. Cover and cook over medium-high until potatoes are done (about 20 minutes). Add beans. Cook for several more minutes and serve. If using salt free beans use 2½ tsp. salt instead of 1¾ tsp.

YIELD: 8 c.

DUTCH POTATO SOUP

2 minced garlic cloves	4 c. water
1 c. chopped onions	¾ c. cashew pieces
3 Tbs. oil	1 c. TOFU COTTAGE
2 tsp. salt	CHEESE
4 c. thinly sliced raw potatoes (packed into cup)	

In small skillet, saute first four ingredients together until onions are clear. (Salt draws juice from onions). In saucepan, bring potatoes and 3 c. of water to boil. Reduce heat and simmer until tender (about 20 minutes). Blend remaining cup of water and cashews on high for 1-2 minutes until creamy. Add to potatoes. Boil for several minutes, stirring constantly. Remove from heat and fold in sauteed onions and TOFU COTTAGE CHEESE. Serve. May garnish with fresh parsley.

YIELD: 7 c.

SALADS, VEGETABLES, SOUPS...

SPRING SOUP

4 c. water
2 c. cubed potatoes, 1"
3 c. fresh cauliflower, 1"
  pieces
1 tsp. garlic powder

2 tsp. salt
1½ Tbs. onion powder
1 Tbs. dried chives or 2 Tbs.
  fresh

Put first three ingredients into pot and bring to boil. Reduce heat to medium, cover and simmer until potatoes and cauliflower are tender (approx. 20 minutes). Remove from heat and blend 3 c. at a time until pureed. Pour into another pot. Repeat procedure until all is blended. Add next three ingredients and stir together. Bring to boil; add chives and serve.

YIELD: 7 c.

TOFU GUMBO SOUP

2 c. crumbed tofu
2 c. chopped onions
1½ tsp. olive oil
¼ c. COUNTRY-STYLE
  SEASONING

3 c. water
2 c. COOKED BROWN RICE
2½ c. chopped zucchini
2½ c. chopped tomatoes

Rinse, drain, crumble and measure tofu. Set aside. In pot, saute onions in olive oil for several minutes. In small bowl, stir together COUNTRY-STYLE SEASONING with ½ c. of water. Add to pot with rest of water and remaining ingredients, including tofu. Bring to boil and cook until zucchini is tender. Serve.

YIELD: 7 c.

SCOTCH BROTH

6 c. water
⅓ c. dry pearled barley
1⅓ c. sliced celery
2¼ c. diced carrots
1 c. chopped onions
½ tsp. garlic powder
1½ Tbs. onion powder
½ tsp. oregano

½ tsp. basil
2 tsp. salt
¾ c. cashew pieces
¾ c. water
1½ tsp. dried parsley
1½ c. frozen green peas

Continued on next page...

Put first 10 ingredients into large pot and bring to boil. Reduce heat, cover and simmer until barley is cooked and vegetables are tender (approx. 1 hour). Blend next two ingredients on high 1-2 minutes until creamy. Rinse peas under hot water and drain. When soup is ready, add cashew cream, parsley and peas. Bring to boil and cook several minutes.
YIELD: 9 c.

KRISTIN'S SERENDIPITY SOUP

2 Tbs. olive oil	1 Tbs. chopped fresh chives or
1 minced garlic clove	scallion tops
1½ tsp. basil	¾ c. tomato puree
1½ tsp. oregano	1 tsp. cumin
1 c. carrot circles, ¼"	1¾ tsp. salt
¼ c. chopped onions	1 Tbs. onion powder
4 c. water	1 tsp. garlic powder
2½ c. cubed potatoes, ½"	⅓ c. pitted black olives, whole
(about 5 small potatoes)	1½ c. frozen green peas
¾ c. shredded white cabbage	1 c. tomato wedges

In large pot, briefly saute first four ingredients on medium-high. Add carrots and onions and saute for 10 minutes, stirring often. Put in next three ingredients and bring to boil. Cook until potatoes are half done (about 10 minutes). Add next seven ingredients and continue cooking until potatoes are tender (about 10 more minutes). Rinse peas under hot water. Drain and add along with tomatoes. Cook for 2-3 more minutes. Serve.
YIELD: 8 c.

BEVERAGES

SUPER SMOOTHIE

1 c. APRICOT NECTAR   **1 c. unsweetened pineapple juice**
1 c. orange juice   **2 bananas, fresh or frozen**

Put all ingredients into blender. Cut bananas into several pieces and add. Blend on high for one minute. Pour into pitcher and serve or chill.

YIELD: 4½ c.

Variations:

1. Omit NECTAR and replace with half orange juice and half pineapple juice.
2. May add other fresh or frozen fruit such as strawberries, blueberries or grapes.

APRICOT NECTAR

1 c. dried apricots, sulphured   **1-2 Tbs. honey**
2 c. water   **1½ c. water**

Bring first two ingredients to boil in saucepan. Remove from heat, cover and set aside for 5 minutes. Then pour into blender and add remaining ingredients. Blend on high for one minute until creamy. Pour into pitcher and chill.

YIELD: 4 c.

GRAPE-BANANA SHAKE

2 c. unsweetened grape juice   **3-4 med. FROZEN BANANAS**

Pour juice into blender. Cut bananas into several pieces and add. Blend on high for 30-60 seconds. Pour into pitcher and serve immediately.

YIELD: Approximately 3¾ c.

BEVERAGES

SOY MILK #1
(from soy beans)

To prepare beans:

1 c. dry soybeans   **½ c. coconut**

Soak beans overnight in about 5 c. cool water. Next morning rinse and drain. (1 c. dry soybeans = approx. 2½ c. soaked) Put soaked soybeans into saucepan with 5 c. water and the coconut. Cover and bring to boil. Reduce heat and simmer for 25 minutes. Immediately remove from heat.

To make milk:

1 c. water   **¼ tsp. salt**
2 Tbs. honey   **3 c. water**
2 tsp. vanilla

Measure 1 c. cooked beans and coconut from saucepan and put into blender. Add all but the last ingredient and blend on high 2-3 minutes until creamy. Stop blender and add remaining water measurement. Blend briefly. Strain milk 2-3 times through cheesecloth or nylon stocking. Pour into pitcher. Repeat above procedure with another cup of beans. Add to pitcher and chill.

YIELD: 2½ qts. soy milk

Note: Milk freezes well. After thawing blend briefly before using.

SOY MILK #2
(from SOY BASE)

½ c. SOY BASE   **2 tsp. vanilla**
½ c. water   **¼ tsp. salt**
¼-⅓ c. oil or ¼ c. cashews   **4 c. water**
2 Tbs. honey

Blend all but last ingredient on high 2-3 minutes, until creamy. Stop blender and add as much of the remaining water (last ingredient) as possible without spilling. Blend briefly. Pour into pitcher with remaining water. Chill.

YIELD: 5 c.

BEVERAGES

SOY BASE

2 c. soy flour   4 c. water

Blend or wisk together ingredients. Cook in a double boiler until a thick paste consistency, about 2 hours. Best used immediately or keep in refrigerator up to 4 days. Or may measure out ½ cup proportions, wrap individually in plastic wrap and freeze.

YIELD: 3¾ c.

Variations: Other methods for cooking include:
1. Crockpot — Cook ingredients on high, covered, 3 hours in crockpot.
2. Simmer ring — Place ring on burner. Place covered sauce pan on ring. Lightly boil ingredients about 30 minutes, stirring occasionally.
3. Oven — Place ingredients in an uncovered 2 quart casserole dish. Bake at 350° for 1 hour. Stir occasionally.

TAHINI-BANANA MILK

2½ c. cool water   1⅓ c. mashed bananas (approx.
⅓ c. tahini   3 medium bananas)
                                      ¼ tsp. salt

Blend all ingredients on high for one minute until creamy. Pour into pitcher and serve immediately. (Bananas will turn milk brown as it sits.)
YIELD: 4½ c.

TAHINI-DATE MILK

1½ c. hot water   2 tsp. vanilla
½ c. coconut   ¼ tsp. salt
½ c. tahini   2 c. cool water
20 pitted dates

Blend all but the last ingredient on high 2-3 minutes until creamy. Stop blender and add remainder of water. Blend for 15 seconds more. Pour into pitcher and serve or chill.
YIELD: 5 c.

BEVERAGES

COCONUT-OAT MILK

1½ c. water	½ c. coconut
12-13 pitted dates	½ tsp. salt
½ c. rolled oats	2 c. water

Put all but the last ingredient into saucepan. Bring to boil. Cover and simmer on low 15-20 minutes, stirring occasionally. Put into blender and add remaining water measurement. Blend on high for one minute until creamy. Pour into pitcher and chill before serving.

YIELD: 4 c.

Variations: May add 2-4 Tbs. carob powder and/or a banana.

BASIC NUT MILK

1 c. water	¼ tsp. salt
1 c. cashew pieces, walnuts, filberts or brazil nuts	1 tsp. vanilla
	3 c. water
1-2 Tbs. honey or 4-8 pitted dates	

Blend all but the last ingredient on high 1-2 minutes until creamy. Stop blender and add remaining water measurement. Blend briefly. Pour into pitcher and serve immediately or chill.

YIELD: 4⅔ c.

Variations: May flavor with fresh or frozen fruit of your choice such as bananas, strawberries, blueberries, etc. Add fruit to other ingredients before blending.

CAROB MILK

1½ c. water	¼ c. carob powder
¾ c. cashew pieces or SOY BASE	½ tsp. coffee substitute
	¼ tsp. salt
8-10 pitted dates or 1 Tbs. honey and 1 tsp. molasses (not blackstrap)	2 tsp. vanilla
	2-3 Tbs. oil if using SOY BASE
	2½ c. water

Blend all but the last ingredient on high 1-2 minutes until creamy. Stop blender and add remaining water measurement. Blend briefly. Pour into pitcher and serve immediately or chill.

YIELD: 4¾ c.

BEVERAGES

STAWBERRY MILK

1 c. water
¾ c. cashew pieces
4-6 pitted dates
1½ tsp. vanilla
⅔ c. frozen apple juice
concentrate

¼ tsp. salt
2¾ c. frozen strawberries #1
1¼ c. frozen strawberries #2

Blend all but the last ingredient on high 1-2 minutes until creamy. Stop blender and add frozen strawberries #2. Blend for 3-5 seconds. Pour into pitcher and serve.

YIELD: 4 c.

MILD MOCHA MILK

1½ c. water
1 c. cashew pieces
8 pitted dates
2 tsp. carob powder

3 Tbs. coffee substitute
¼ tsp. salt
½ tsp. maple flavoring
2½ c. water

Blend all but the last ingredient on high 1-2 minutes until creamy. Stop blender and add remaining water measurement. Blend briefly. Pour into pitcher and serve or chill.

YIELD: 4⅔ c.

CASHEW BANANA-PINEAPPLE MILK

3 c. unsweetened pineapple
juice
¾ c. cashew pieces

¼ tsp. salt
2 large, ripe bananas

Blend 1 c. of juice with cashews and salt on high 1-2 minutes until creamy. Stop blender and add remainder of juice and bananas cut into several pieces. Blend another minute on high. Pour into pitcher and serve or chill.

YIELD: 4¾ c.

BEVERAGES

CASHEW-PEAR MILK

1 c. water
1 c. cashew pieces
2 Tbs. honey (optional)
1 tsp. vanilla

¼ tsp. salt
3 c. canned pears (measured with juice)

Blend all but the last ingredient on high 1-2 minutes until creamy. Stop blender and add pears. Blend for 30 seconds more. Pour into pitcher and serve or chill.

YIELD: 4¾ c.

HALF AND HALF

1½ c. water
½ c. cashew pieces
½ c. BLANCHED ALMONDS
2 Tbs. honey

½ tsp. vanilla (optional)
¼ tsp. salt
2½ c. water

Blend all but the last ingredient on high 1-2 minutes until creamy. Stop blender and add remaining water measurement. Blend briefly. Pour into pitcher and serve immediately or chill.

YIELD: 4¾ c.

Note: May strain after blending for a creamier consistency.

ALMOND MILK SUPREME

1½ c. water
1 c. BLANCHED ALMONDS
2 Tbs. honey
½ tsp. vanilla

¼ tsp. almond flavoring
¼ tsp. salt
2 c. water

Blend all but the last ingredient on high 1-2 minutes until creamy. Stop blender and add remaining water measurement. Blend briefly. Pour into pitcher and serve immediately or chill.

YIELD: 4¼ c.

Note: May strain after blending for a creamier consistency.

BEVERAGES

ALMOND COCONUT MILK

1½ c. hot water
½ c. **TOASTED COCONUT**
½ c. **TOASTED ALMONDS**
3 Tbs. honey

¼ tsp. coconut flavoring
¼ tsp. almond flavoring
¼ tsp. salt
2½ c. water

Blend all but the last ingredient on high 1-2 minutes until creamy. Stop blender and add remaining water measurement. Blend briefly. Pour into pitcher and chill before serving.
YIELD: 4¾ c.

BANANA HAZELNUT MILK

1½ c. water
¾ c. **TOASTED HAZELNUTS**
      (filberts)
6-8 pitted dates

1½ tsp. vanilla
2 medium bananas
¼ tsp. salt
2½ c. water

Blend all but the last ingredient on high 1-2 minutes until creamy. Stop blender and add remaining water measurement. Blend briefly. Pour into pitcher and serve or chill.
YIELD: 5⅓ c.

CAROB HAZELNUT MILK

2 c. water
⅔ c. **TOASTED HAZELNUTS**
      (filberts)
15 pitted dates
3 Tbs. carob powder

2 tsp. vanilla
½ tsp. coffee substitute
¼ tsp. salt
2 c. water

Blend all but the last ingredient on high 1-2 minutes until creamy. Stop blender and add remaining water measurement. Blend briefly. Pour into pitcher and serve or chill.
YIELD: 5 c.

BEVERAGES

BANANA WALNUT MILK

1½ c. water	2 medium bananas
¾ c. **TOASTED WALNUTS**	¼ tsp. salt
1 Tbs. honey	2½ c. water

Blend all but the last ingredient on high 1-2 minutes until creamy. Stop blender and add remaining water measurement. Blend briefly. Pour into pitcher and serve or chill.

YIELD: 5¼ c.

MAPLE WALNUT MILK

1½ c. water	2¼ tsp. maple flavoring
¾ c. **TOASTED WALNUTS**	¼ tsp. salt
15 pitted dates	2½ c. water

Blend all but the last ingredient on high 1-2 minutes until creamy. Stop blender and add remaining water measurement. Blend briefly. Pour into pitcher and serve or chill.

YIELD: 4¾ c.

FIGGIE MILK

9 calimyrna or Turkish dried figs	4 c. **BASIC NUT MILK** or **SOY MILK**

Remove stems and cut figs in half. Add to blender along with milk. Blend on high 2-3 minutes until creamy. Pour into pitcher and serve or chill.

YIELD: 4½ c.

Variation: For thicker milk, add 5-6 more figs.

BEVERAGES

SWEET CASHEW MILK

1 c. cashew pieces
4 c. water
¼ c. honey or ½ c. DATE
      BUTTER
2 tsp. vanilla

¼ tsp. salt
1 tsp. coriander
1 tsp. grated orange rind
⅛ tsp. anise (optional)

Blend cashews and 1 c. water on high 1-2 minutes until creamy. Stop blender and add remaining ingredients. Blend 15 more seconds. Use in OLD-FASHIONED BREAD PUDDING.

YIELD: 4½ c.

BREADS

OAT CRACKERS

2 c. whole wheat flour
1½ c. rolled oats
1 c. OAT FLOUR

1¼ tsp. salt
1¼ c. water
¾ c. oil

In bowl stir together first four ingredients. Blend last two ingredients on high for 30 seconds. Pour into flours and mix all together well. Divide in half and roll each piece out on cookie sheet. Score. Bake at 350° for 15-20 minutes.
YIELD: 2 - 18" x 12" cookie sheets or 70 - 1⅝" x 1¾" crackers.

SESAME SOUP THINS

½ c. water
6 Tbs. oil
½ tsp. salt

2 c. whole wheat flour
½ c. sesame seeds

Blend first three ingredients on high for 30 seconds. Pour into bowl and add remaining ingredients. Stir together well and knead briefly. Set aside for 10 minutes. Then place on cookie sheet and roll out. Sprinkle with salt and a generous amount of sesame seeds. Roll seeds into dough. Score. Bake at 350° for 15-20 minutes.
YIELD: 1- 15" x 18" cookie sheet or about 72 - 2" x 1⅛" crackers.

GRAHAM CRACKERS

⅓ c. oil
⅓ c. honey
¾ c. OAT FLOUR

1¼ c. whole wheat pastry flour
1½ tsp. coriander
¼ tsp. salt

In small bowl beat together first two ingredients with fork. In another bowl stir together remaining ingredients. Pour liquid into dry ingredients and mix together well. Put dough on cookie sheet and flatten. Cover with plastic wrap and roll out dough. Score. Bake at 350° for 8 minutes.
YIELD: 1 - 18" x 12" pan or 44 - 1½" x 3" crackers.

BREADS

CORN JOURNEY CAKES

½ c. raisins
2 c. hot water
2 Tbs. oil
6 Tbs. honey
2 tsp. vanilla (optional)

2 c. unrefined cornmeal
2 c. OAT FLOUR
¾ c. coconut
1 tsp. salt

In small bowl let raisins soak in water for 10 minutes. Add next three ingredients and beat together briefly with fork. In another bowl stir together remaining ingredients. Pour liquid ingredients into dry ingredients and mix together well. Let sit 10 minutes. Put ¼ c. portions on LECITHIN-OILED cookie sheet, flatten with fork and shape. Bake at 325° for 50-55 minutes until golden brown on bottom of cakes.
YIELD: 20 - ¼ c. cakes

INGREDIENTS FOR BREADMAKING

FLOUR

Hard, red kernel wheat ground into a fine flour is the best in breadmaking. It has a high gluten content which enables it to expand and hold the gas given off by the yeast and warm water.

Flour varies in moisture content depending on the weather and method of storage of flour. Moisture variations affect the way the flour absorbs. Therefore, amounts of flour in recipes are not exact. When adding flour, be on the safe side and add smaller amounts of flour first, and then just enough to make a moist and very slightly sticky dough. Remember: Whole wheat bread dough, unlike white bread, will always be slightly sticky even when the right amount of flour has been added.

When measuring flour, it is best to spoon into a measuring cup and level with a knife. Do not pack down or shake the cup.

Experiment with the versatile BASIC WHOLE WHEAT BREAD RECIPE. Put whole wheat flour in the limelight, but share the stage with the other flours or cooked whole grain cereals. See the following list for ideas.

1. When adding cooked whole grains to bread dough reduce the amount of liquid in the recipe.

2. Rye flour provides stickiness but lacks gluten which provides elasticity. Use rye in small amounts.

3. To reduce graininess in corn bread, mix the cornmeal and liquid in the recipe, bring to a boil and cool before mixing with the other ingredients.

Continued on next page...

4. Oatmeal is better if soaked in very hot water and cooled before the yeast is added.

5. Soy flour is an excellent addition to whole grain bread. It adds moistness to bread. However, too much will cause heavy bread. A good ratio is ¼-½ cup soy flour to 3 cups whole wheat flour.

6. Soft wheat flour, or pastry flour, has a low gluten content. It will cause bread to be crumbly. Works well in quick breads and pastries.

YEAST

Yeasts are living organisms which feed on sugars and produce alcohol and carbon dioxide, the gas which enables bread to rise. Yet yeast depends on proper environmental conditions to bring it to life. These conditions are proper liquid temperature and the presence of simple sugar or starch. The liquid temperature that best activates dry yeast is 110° to 115°. This is a warm temperature but not hot. Yeast begins to die when the temperature hits around 120°. Small quantities of simple sugars speed the yeast action, while too much slows it down.

In breadmaking, yeast is the most wholesome leavening agent. Baking soda and baking powder are not essential. These agents are harmful to the human system as they irritate the stomach lining and are destructive to B vitamins.

Use fresh yeast. Old or improperly stored yeast will often not rise. Yeast will keep several months in the freezer, a few months in the refrigerator but only a few weeks at room temperature. To determine if yeast is fresh and active see point number 1c under PROCEDURE FOR BREADMAKING. Too much yeast makes bread distasteful.

Yeast can be purchased in bulk through natural food outlets. This is much cheaper than buying small, prewrapped packages in supermarkets.

SALT AND OIL

Salt and oil enhance the flavor of bread, giving a richer taste and added tenderness. Salt is also a yeast control, keeping the yeast from running wild. However, proper timing is important when adding these ingredients to bread. The yeast mixture should be completely dissolved and appear bubbly. When using the sponge method, the gluten should be developed before adding these flavor enhancers. Remember — too much salt inhibits the action of the yeast. Oil, though it adds a richer flavor and tenderness, is not essential.

Continued on next page...

BREADS

PROCEDURE FOR BREADMAKING

1. MIXING

   a. Read directions carefully.

   b. Assemble ingredients in work area beforehand. It is best that the flour and utensils are at room temperature; if these are cold, they can slow the action of the yeast.

   c. Prepare to dissolve yeast by adding the liquid at the right temperature (warm) and a small quantity of sweetener. If the yeast is good it will dissolve and appear bubbly in 10 minutes.

   d. Next, add whole wheat flour, one cup at a time, beating vigorously to incorporate air which develops the gluten. In the Sponge Dough Technique, a partial quantity of flour is added and then set in a covered bowl in a warm place. In 15 to 30 minutes the dough will take on the characteristics of its name as it becomes foamy and spongy with unbroken air bubbles.

   e. Beat the mixture down and add salt, oil and/or lecithin. This is also the time to add more sweetener, if desired, raisins, dates, cooked cereals, sprouted grains or seeds, nuts, or other whole grain flours.

   f. Add just enough flour, one cup at a time, until the dough leaves the sides of the bowl.

2. KNEADING

   a. Place dough on a floured counter top and begin to knead. To knead, fold dough up with fingers and press and fold down with the heels of hands. Turn 90 degrees and repeat this process for 10 minutes until dough is moist, soft and elastic. The most important aspect of the first kneading is that it be done thoroughly. The more definite and rhythmic in kneading, the finer the crumb will be.

   d. If dough is hard to handle, lightly oil hands or briefly rinse hands under a faucet every now and then.

3. RAISING

   a. After kneading, place dough in a clean, lightly oiled bowl. Cover bowl with towel to prevent the dough from drying out.

   b. Next is the rising or proofing stage, where the dough rises double in bulk. Do not permit it to rise more than double, for if it falls back the bread will be coarser and drier. The object of this stage is to attain a light and moist crumb.

Continued on next page . . .

BREADS

c. The environment plays an important role in the proofing. The room needs to be free from drafts. The bread dough will rise nicely in a 75-80 degree area. When the dough has sufficiently risen (30-60 minutes), punch down and knead a few minutes in the bowl. Note how much easier it handles.

4. SHAPING INTO PAN

a. Divide dough into the number of pieces stated in the recipe. Do not pull or stretch dough apart. Take a piece of dough and slap it on the board to free the trapped air bubbles. Roll with a rolling pin or use hands to shape into a rectangle. Start at narrow end and roll up tightly, like a jelly roll. Place dough in oiled pans making sure the dough touches the edges of the pan so it will support the loaf as it rises.

b. To grease pans, use LECITHIN-OIL mixture. Oil, used alone, may result in sticking.

c. Cover with towel and return to a warm place to rise until almost double in bulk.

d. Avoid drafts and heavy trafficking (running and jumping) for dough might fall.

e. When dough is rising in bread pan do not let it over proof (raise too long). Make a slight indentation with finger, if the impression still remains this is good. Bread can be baked safely without falling.

5. BAKING DIRECTIONS

a. Bake bread at 350° in preheated oven unless directions state otherwise. Bake for 35-45 minutes until golden brown or as directed in the recipe.

6. CHECK FOR DONENESS

a. Bread should be thoroughly baked. Yet the question often arises, "How does one know that the bread is done?" Here are some suggestions:

— Bake bread in smaller loaf pans.

— A well baked loaf should shrink a little while it bakes and easily fall out of a well seasoned pan.

— The bottom of a well baked loaf will not burn the palm of hand when placed there right from oven.

— The bread should sound hollow when tapped on the bottom.

Continued on next page...

b. Thoroughly cool bread before wrapping and storing; otherwise, condensation will appear, making bread wet and more likely to mold.

7. WHEN TO EAT

    a. Yeast bread is best eaten one to three days later. When taken fresh out of the oven there are still harmful substances left in the bread from the fermentation process. However, these substances will evaporate in a day or two, thus leaving the bread easier to digest and more nourishing.

COMMON DEFECTS OF BREAD AND POSSIBLE CAUSES

1. SOUR TASTE

    a. Water too warm.
    b. Period rising too long. Punch down and reshape if it has been rising more than 60 minutes.
    c. Temperature too high while rising.
    d. Poor yeast.

2. DRY OR CRUMBLY

    a. Too much flour in dough.
    b. Over-baking.

3. HEAVINESS

    a. Unevenness of temperature while rising.
    b. Insufficient kneading.
    c. Old flour.
    d. Old yeast.

4. CRACKS IN CRUST

    a. Baking before sufficiently light.
    b. Oven too hot at first.

5. TOO THICK A CRUST

    a. Oven too slow.
    b. Baked too long.
    c. Excess of salt.

Continued on next page...

BREADS

6. DARK PATCHES OR STREAKS

   a. Shortening added to flour before liquid, thus allowing flour particles to become coated with fat before they had mixed evenly with the liquid.

7. SOGGINESS

   a. Too much liquid.
   b. Insufficient baking.
   c. Cooling in airtight container.

8. ILL-SHAPED LOAF

   a. Not molded well originally.
   b. Too large a loaf for the pan.
   c. Rising period too long.
   d. Loaves flat on top may result from inadequate kneading.

9. HOLES IN BREAD

   a. Dough not sufficiently kneaded, should knead 8 to 10 minutes.
   b. Before shaping dough into loaves, make sure gas bubbles are kneaded out.
   c. Do not let dough proof too long or too fast in the baking pans. When the loaf hits the heat of the preheated oven it will rise a little more.

BASIC WHOLE WHEAT BREAD

4 c. warm water
2 Tbs. dry yeast
⅓ c. honey
2 c. whole wheat flour
¼ c. oil

1 Tbs. salt
2 Tbs. lecithin (optional)
(when using lecithin may omit oil)
7-7½ c. whole wheat flour

In large bowl stir together first four ingredients to make sponge. Let bubble in warm place for 15-20 minutes. Stir in oil and salt. Then mix in most of remaining flour until it becomes difficult to stir. Turn dough onto board or counter and knead in remainder of flour. Knead well (up to ten minutes). When texture is correct, dough should be slightly sticky and spring back when lightly pressed. Put back into bowl, cover and let rise in warm place until just about double in size. Punch down and knead briefly in bowl. Cut into three equal pieces. Knead each piece on lightly oiled

Continued on next page...

BREADS

board or counter. Shape into loaves and place in LECITHIN-OILED pans. Cover and let rise again in pans in warm place until not quite double in size. Bake at 350° for 40-45 minutes. Remove from pans and allow to cool standing on end or on cooling rack.

YIELD: 3 medium loaves (1¼-1½#) 8½" x 4½" x 2½"

Variation: May replace ½ c. whole wheat flour with ½ c. soy flour.

DILLY BREAD

2 Tbs. water	4 tsp. salt
2 Tbs. olive oil	½ c. cornmeal
2 c. onions, chopped	¼ c. yeast flakes
2 c. warm water	3½ Tbs. dill seed, ground or ¼ c.
2 Tbs. dry yeast	dill weed
⅓ c. honey	1 c. white flour (unbleached)
⅓ c. oil	5-5½ c. whole wheat flour

Saute first three ingredients. In separate bowl mix next three ingredients. Let sit 10 minutes, until yeast bubbles. After yeast bubbles add 2 cups whole wheat flour. Stir vigorously for 1-2 minutes. Place in warm place and let rise until double, about 20 minutes. To this yeast/flour mixture stir in well the next six ingredients plus the onions. Then add remaining whole wheat flour, beating in one cup at a time until dough is slightly sticky but can be kneaded. Knead well for about 3-5 minutes. Place in a clean, oiled bowl and cover with towel. Let rise until double, about 30-40 minutes. Punch down and knead. Divide into 2 parts and shape. Place in LECITHIN-OILED pans. Let rise again until double. Preheat oven to 350° and bake bread 45 minutes.

YIELD: 2 medium loaves, 8½" x 4½" x 2½"

RAISIN PUMPERNICKEL

2 c. cold water	½ c. warm water
½ c. cornmeal	2 tsp. honey
2 tsp. salt	2 Tbs. dry yeast
2 Tbs. oil	1 c. rye flour
¼ c. molasses	5-6 c. whole wheat flour
1 c. raisins	

Continued on next page...

BREADS

Place first two ingredients in saucepan. Bring to boil, stirring constantly until thickened, about 5 minutes. Remove from heat and stir in next 4 ingredients. Set this aside to cool for about 20 minutes, stirring occasionally. In a separate bowl combine next 3 ingredients. Let sit until yeast bubbles, about 10 minutes. Then add cornmeal mixture and rye flour to yeast mixture. Then add, one cup at a time, whole wheat flour to make a soft dough that can be kneaded. Knead well, about 3-5 minutes. Place in a clean, oiled bowl and cover with towel. Let rise until double, about 30-40 minutes. Punch down and knead. Divide into 2 parts and shape. Place in LECITHIN-OILED pans. Let rise again until double. Preheat oven to 350° and bake bread 45 minutes.

YIELD: 2 medium loaves, 8½" x 4½" x 2½"

DARK PEASANT BREAD

1½ c. very warm water	2 tsp. caraway seeds
2 Tbs. dry yeast	1 tsp. salt
¼ c. molasses	¼ c. carob powder, sifted
1 c. rye flour	(optional)
2 Tbs. oil (optional)	3-4 c. whole wheat flour

Combine and dissolve first three ingredients and let sit until bubbly, about 10 minutes. Beat in well two cups whole wheat flour. Place in warm area until double in bulk, about 20 minutes. Stir in next five ingredients. Then add, one cup at a time, whole wheat flour to make a soft dough that can be kneaded. Knead well, about 3-5 minutes. Place in a clean, oiled bowl and cover with towel. Let rise until double, about 30-40 minutes. Punch down and knead. Shape into loaf and place in LECITHIN-OILED pan. Let rise again until double. Preheat oven to 350° and bake 40-45 minutes.

YIELD: 1 large loaf

DELICIOUS OATMEAL BREAD

1½ c. hot water	¼ c. honey
1½ c. rolled oats	3 Tbs. oil
2 Tbs. dry yeast	2 tsp. salt
2 c. warm water	7-7½ c. whole wheat flour

Continued on next page...

BREADS

In small bowl combine first two ingredients. In another bowl briskly stir together next three ingredients plus two cups of the flour. Let stand 15 minutes. After waiting 15 minutes combine all ingredients together except flour. Stir flour in one cup at a time. Make a soft dough that can be kneaded. Turn onto floured board or counter, knead until smooth, about 10 minutes. Place dough in a clean, oiled bowl, cover and let rise in a warm place until double in size, about 30 minutes. Then punch down, knead and divide into two loaves. Place in LECITHIN-OILED pans. Cover and let rise until almost double in size. Bake at 350° for 40-45 minutes.

YIELD: 2 medium loaves, 8½" x 4½" x 2½"

POPPY SEED BREAD

1½ c. rolled oats	¼ c. honey
1 c. hot water	⅓ c. sesame seeds
1¼ c. warm water	⅓ c. sunflower seeds
¼ c. honey	⅓ c. poppy seeds
2 Tbs. dry yeast	2 tsp. salt
2 c. whole wheat flour	3-4 c. whole wheat flour
⅓ c. oil	

Place first two ingredients in bowl and set aside. Briskly mix together next four ingredients, let sit 15 minutes. After waiting 15 minutes stir together well all ingredients except the last one. Add remaining flour, one cup at a time, making a soft dough. Place dough on floured board or counter. Knead approximately 5-10 minutes. Place in bowl, covered, in a warm place. Let rise until double, about 30 minutes. Then punch down, knead and shape into two loaves. Place into two LECITHIN-OILED pans. Cover and let rise until almost double, about 20-30 minutes. Bake at 350° 40-45 minutes.

YIELD: 2 medium loaves, 8½" x 4½" x 2½"

HERB & GARLIC BREAD

½ c. chopped onion	1 Tbs. honey
2 finely chopped garlic cloves	1½ tsp. salt
3 Tbs. oil	1½ tsp. thyme
1½ c. warm water	1 tsp. sage
1 Tbs. dry yeast	4-5 c. whole wheat flour

Continued on next page...

BREADS

Saute first three ingredients then set aside to partially cool. In a large mixing bowl stir together next three ingredients and let bubble 10 minutes. Stir together well all but flour. Add flour one cup at a time, making a soft dough. Place dough on floured board or counter. Knead approximately 5-10 minutes. Place in bowl, covered, in a warm place. Let rise until double, about 30 minutes. Then punch down, knead and shape into one loaf. Place into a LECITHIN-OILED pan. Cover and let rise until almost double, about 20-30 minutes. Bake at 350° for 45-50 minutes.

YIELD: 1 large loaf

ONE LOAF RECIPE FOR CHILDREN

1 c. warm water	1 tsp. salt
1 Tbs. honey	1 Tbs. oil
2 tsp. dry yeast	2-2½ c. whole wheat flour
½ c. whole wheat flour	

In bowl stir together first four ingredients to make sponge. Let bubble for 15-20 minutes. Stir in oil and salt, then flour. Turn onto oiled board or counter and knead well. Shape into loaf and place in LECITHIN-OILED pan. Cover and let rise in warm place until double in size, about 20-30 minutes. Bake at 350° for 35-45 minutes.

YIELD: 1 medium loaf (1¼-1½#), 8½" x 4½" x 2½"

HOLIDAY FRUIT - NUT BREAD

1 recipe ONE LOAF RECIPE FOR CHILDREN	½ c. chopped walnuts
	½ c. raisins
1 Tbs. honey	½ c. chopped dates
1½ tsp. coriander	½ c. chopped apricots

Follow preparation for ONE LOAF RECIPE FOR CHILDREN. After sponge is completed stir in all the ingredients above. Then work in remaining flour. Bake at 350° for 40-45 minutes.

YIELD: 1 medium loaf (1¼-1½#), 8½" x 4½" x 2½"

BREADS

APPLE ICING BREAD

1 recipe **ONE LOAF RECIPE**
FOR CHILDREN
6-7 c. **applesauce**

½ c. **coconut**
1 c. **chopped dates**
½ c. **chopped nuts**

Follow preparation for ONE LOAF RECIPE FOR CHILDREN. Instead of shaping into loaf, roll dough out on oiled board or counter into 19" x 13" rectangle, ¼" thick. Flip over onto LECITHIN-OILED 18" x 12" cookie sheet. Press dough lightly into corners of pan and shape edges. Let rise in a warm place 20 minutes. Slightly warm applesauce in a saucepan. When dough has risen, fill with applesauce and sprinkle on coconut, dates and nuts. Bake at 350° for 40-45 minutes.

YIELD: 1 - 18" x 12" pan

Variation: May top with ½ c. raisins or 1-2 Tbs. poppy seeds.

HONEY BUNS

1 c. **finely chopped nuts**
½ c. **coconut, ground**
1 tsp. **coriander**

½ c. **honey**
1 recipe **ONE LOAF RECIPE**
FOR CHILDREN

Mix together first three ingredients. Pour honey into separate small bowl. Follow preparation for ONE LOAF RECIPE FOR CHILDREN. Form the dough into ¼ c. balls by rolling each one on a floured board in a circular motion. Then roll each ball in honey then in nut mixture. Place balls in an oiled 9" round cake pan. Let rise 20 minutes in a warm place. Bake at 350° for 35-40 minutes or until golden brown.

YIELD: 13-15 buns

BREADS

PECAN ROLLS

1 recipe **ONE LOAF RECIPE FOR CHILDREN**	½ c. **water**
¾ c. **DATE BUTTER #1**	¼ c. **honey**
1 c. **chopped pecans or walnuts**	¼ c. **oil**
	¼ c. **DATE BUTTER #2**

Follow preparation for ONE LOAF RECIPE FOR CHILDREN, doubling the honey. After kneading the dough, roll into 13" x 16" rectangle. Spread DATE BUTTER #1 on dough. Start at one of the sides measuring 13" and roll up like a jelly roll. Cut off the uneven ends. Cut into 1" slices. Mix together remaining ingredients and pour into the bottom of a 9" round cake pan. Place slices face down in the pan. Let rise until double, about 20 minutes. Bake at 350° for 35-40 minutes or until golden brown.
YIELD: 13-15 rolls

DANISHES

1 recipe **ONE LOAF RECIPE FOR CHILDREN**	1½ c. **DATE BUTTER**
	½ c. **chopped nuts, i.e. walnuts**

Follow preparation for ONE LOAF RECIPE FOR CHILDREN, doubling the honey. Roll into 19" x 13" rectangle, ¼" thick, on oiled counter or cutting board. Spread DATE BUTTER to within ½" of edges and sprinkle with chopped nuts. Start at one of the sides measuring 13" and roll up like a jelly roll. Press seams together. Cut into 1¼" slices and place face up on LECITHIN-OILED cookie sheet. Let rise 10-15 minutes. Bake at 350° for 25-30 minutes. May glace with unsweetened orange juice concentrate while still hot from the oven.
YIELD: Approximately 10 danishes
Variation: May use other dried fruit butters.

WHOLE WHEAT FRENCH BREAD

1 c. **warm water**	1 Tbs. **oil**
2 tsp. **honey**	2¼ c. **whole wheat flour**
2 tsp. **dry yeast**	¾ tsp. **salt**

Continued on next page...

BREADS

In small bowl stir together first three ingredients. Let bubble 10 minutes. Then briefly stir in oil. In another bowl stir together flour and salt. Make a hole in center of flour and pour in liquid mixture. Stir together but do not knead. The dough will be soft. Cover with damp cloth and set in a warm place to let rise 1½ hours. Punch dough down. Place on floured board or counter and pat into rectangle. Form into French loaf by starting at one of the more narrow sides and begin to roll. Continue rolling and pressing outward with hands, tapering dough towards the ends until a long thin form results. Place loaf on LECITHIN-OILED cookie sheet. Cut diagonal, ¼" deep slits across the top with sharp-pointed scissors. Set in warm place to rise until double in size, about 20 minutes. On bottom of oven place a pan filled ½" deep with very hot water. Bake 15 minutes at 400°. Reduce heat to 350° and continue baking 30 minutes longer. Remove from oven and lightly brush loaf with vegetable oil.

YIELD: 1 French loaf

CORN BREAD

2 c.	warm water	
1 Tbs.	dry yeast	
¼ c.	honey	
2½ c.	unrefined cornmeal	
1 c.	whole wheat flour	

1 c.	OAT FLOUR, whole wheat pastry or unbleached white flour
1½ tsp.	salt
¼ c.	oil

In small bowl stir together first three ingredients. Let bubble for 10 minutes. In another bowl stir together remaining ingredients. Combine all ingredients and stir. Put into LECITHIN-OILED 8" x 12" baking dish and let rise in warm place until just below top of dish. This takes about 15 minutes. Bake at 350° for 40 minutes or until golden brown.

YIELD: 1 - 8" x 12" pan of corn bread

Variation: May add 1 c. chopped dates and ½ c. chopped walnuts to flour.

DELICIOUS BISCUITS

1¼ c.	warm water
2 Tbs.	dry yeast
2 tsp.	honey
1½ c.	OAT FLOUR or whole wheat pastry flour

1½ c.	whole wheat flour
1 tsp.	salt
⅓ c.	oil

Continued on next page...

BREADS

Mix together first three ingredients and let bubble 10 minutes. In another bowl stir together next three ingredients. After yeast mixture has sat add dry ingredients and oil. Mix well. Dough will be sticky. Roll out dough ⅜" thick on floured surface. Cut out biscuits with top of a glass. Place on LECITHIN-OILED cookie sheet. Let rise in warm place 10 minutes. Bake at 350° for 25 minutes or until golden brown. Delicious topped with COUNTRY STYLE GRAVY or CHIPPED TOFU. Best served one or two days after baking.

YIELD: 10 - 2½" biscuits.

ENGLISH SCONES

Make one recipe of DELICIOUS BISCUITS using SWEET CASHEW MILK in place of water. Add 1 c. dried fruit (chopped if using large fruit) to dry ingredients. Raisins are traditional. Delicious served with SUPPER FRUIT SOUP.

YIELD: 12 - 3" scones or 18 - 2" scones

RYE MUFFINS

½ c. hot water	¼ c. soy flour, cornmeal or
¾ c. raisins	oat bran
½ c. warm water	1 Tbs. molasses (not blackstrap)
1 Tbs. dry yeast	2 tsp. vanilla
2 Tbs. honey	½ tsp. salt
1 c. rye flour	3 Tbs. oil (optional)
¾ c. OAT FLOUR	

Put first two ingredients in small bowl and set aside. Stir together next three ingredients in another small bowl and let bubble. After yeast mixture has bubbled 10 minutes stir together all ingredients in recipe including the raisins and water they soaked in. Put ⅓ c. portions into LECITHIN-OILED muffin tins. Let rise in warm place 5-7 minutes. Bake at 350° for 30-35 minutes. Cool for 5 minutes before removing from pan.

YIELD: 8 - ⅓ c. muffins

Variation: May use chopped dates or blueberries in place of raisins

BREADS

BLUEBERRY MUFFINS

½ c. warm water
2 Tbs. dry yeast
1 Tbs. honey
1½ c. whole wheat flour
1 c. OAT FLOUR
1 c. whole wheat pastry or
   unbleached white flour

1¼ tsp. salt
1 c. water
½ c. honey
½ c. oil
1 Tbs. vanilla
2 c. frozen blueberries

In small bowl stir together first three ingredients. Set aside to bubble for 5-7 minutes. In another bowl stir together next four ingredients. Blend next four liquids on high for 30 seconds. Pour into dry ingredients. Add yeast mixture when ready. Stir together well. Gently fold in blueberries. Batter should not be runny. Put ⅓ c. portions into LECITHIN-OILED muffin tins. Let rise 5-7 minutes. Bake at 350° for 35 minutes.
YIELD: 17 - ⅓ c. muffins

Variations:

1. APPLE MUFFINS: Replace ½ c. water with ½ c. unsweetened apple juice concentrate. Add 1¼ tsp. coriander and ¼ tsp. anise to dry ingredients. Replace blueberries with 2 c. raw shredded apples. (Press out juice after shredding apples.)
YIELD: 20 - ⅓ c. muffins

2. BANANA-WALNUT MUFFINS: Add 1 c. chopped walnuts and 1½ tsp. grated orange rind to dry ingredients. Use 2¼ c. whole wheat flour instead of 1½ c. Replace blueberries with 2 c. mashed bananas.
YIELD: 22 - ⅓ c. muffins

3. CAROB MUFFINS: Replace ½ c. pastry flour with ½ c. carob powder. Add 1½ c. chopped dates, 1 tsp. coffee substitute and ¾ c. chopped walnuts to dry ingredients.
YIELD: 20 - ⅓ c. muffins

4. POPPY SEED MUFFINS: Add ½ c. poppy seeds and 1 Tbs. grated lemon rind to dry ingredients.
YIELD: 17 - ⅓ c. muffins

BREADS

DELICIOUS DATE MUFFINS

½ c. warm water
2 Tbs. dry yeast
1 tsp. honey
2 c. hot water
1½ c. chopped dates
3½ c. whole wheat flour

2 c. rolled oats
2 tsp. salt
1-1½ tsp. coriander (optional)
½ c. oil
1 Tbs. vanilla

In small bowl stir together first three ingredients and let bubble for 10 minutes. In another bowl mix together remaining ingredients. When yeast mixture is ready, add to rest of ingredients and stir all together. Put ⅓ c. portions into LECITHIN-OILED muffin tins. Let rise 5-7 minutes. Bake at 350° for 35 minutes. Or may fill muffin tins and bake immediately at 400° without letting muffins rise. After 5 minutes reduce heat to 350° and continue baking for 25-30 minutes.

YIELD: 15 - ⅓ c. muffins

ZWIEBACK

Translated from German to English, zwieback means "twice-baked". Use any kind of yeast bread except cracked wheat. Lay slices on oven rack. Bake at 200 for 1½-3 hours until dry. Some breads dry faster due to lightness or thinness. Watch for burning. If using a gas oven the pilot light may be sufficient to dry the bread overnight.

POTPOURRI

AGAR FLAKES & STICK: Agar is a vegetable gelatin. It is often sold in natural food stores in the form of a stick. To make stick into flakes, break into four pieces. Place two pieces in blender, cover and blend on high 15-20 seconds, until flake consistency, not powdery. Repeat procedure. Keep in covered container.

BLANCHED ALMONDS: Drop whole almonds into boiling water for not more than one minute or they will discolor. Pour into colander and rinse under cold water. Drain. Pop off skins and discard.

BREAD CRUMBS: Break one slice of whole grain bread into four pieces. Place in blender, cover and blend on high 15 seconds. Yield is ¾ c. crumbs.

CINNAMON SUBSTITUTE: In small bowl stir together 2 Tbs. coriander and 2 tsp. anise, ground. Store in covered container.

DEXTRINIZED GRAINS: Put uncooked grains into dry skillet not more than 1" deep. Stir constantly over medium high heat until grains are golden and emit a nutty aroma. Immediately remove from skillet. Dextrinized grains cook more quickly, kernals are fluffier, and the flavor is enhanced.

FROZEN BANANAS: Peel ripe but not mushy bananas. Cut or break into 3" pieces. Place in plastic bag until bag is about half full. Expell air and seal bag. Freeze solid, several hours. A table knife is convenient to use to break apart frozen bananas when ready to use. Only take out the bananas to be used for when bananas are left out and begin to soften they take on a darker shade.

GROUND TAPIOCA: Blend ½ c. minute tapioca on high for 15 seconds. Stop blender and stir. Blend again on high for 15 seconds, stop and stir. Repeat this procedure two to three more times. When finished, tapioca will be a mixture of powder and granules. May also use seed grinder for finer consistency.

LECITHIN-OIL SLICKER: This is a replacement for products such as Pam, a food release spray. Pour 6 parts oil, not olive, peanut or sunflower, into a jar with 1 part liquid lecithin. Cover tightly and shake well. Keep at room temperature. Do not use lecithin granules. Measure oil first then use the same utensil to measure lecithin to help prevent sticking of lecithin on utensil.

POTPOURRI

OAT FLOUR: Blend 2 c. quick or rolled oats on high 15-30 seconds, until fine. While blender is running guide oats with a rubber spatula to the center of blender. Store in covered container. Yield is 1⅓ c. flour. If using in recipe immediately after blending tap storage container several times to allow flour to settle (to release air from blending) before measuring.

SOAKED SOYBEANS: Sort and wash beans. Soak 6 to 8 hours in at least three times as much water as beans. In warm weather soak in refrigerator. Rinse and drain. Store in covered container. Will keep in refrigerator for one week or may store in freezer until ready to use.

SOYAGEN: A commercial soy milk powder sold at most natural food stores.

TOASTED NUTS & SEEDS: Place nuts or seeds on cookie sheet and toast at 250° for the following approximate times: Almonds – 2 hours; Brazil Nuts - 1 hour 40 minutes; Cashews - 1 hour 30 minutes; Coconut - 25 minutes; Filberts (Hazelnuts) - 1 hour; Peanuts - 2 hours; Pecans - 1 hour 20 minutes; Walnuts - 1 hour; Pumpkin Seeds (Pepita) - 1 hour 20 minutes; Sesame Seeds - 1 hour 20 minutes; Sunflower Seeds - 1 hour 30 minutes. Toasting enhances the flavor of most nuts and seeds without the use of oil. Note: Coconut and sesame seeds may also be toasted by placing in dry skillet not more than 1" deep. Stir constantly over medium high until sesame seeds crackle or coconut is slightly browned. Remove from skillet immediately.

WHOLE GRAIN PASTA: All pasta should be added to a large amount of rapidly boiling water to ensure that the boiling is not disturbed and pasta has room to cook. Stirring is not necessary when following this method. An approximate guideline is 5-6 parts water to 1 part pasta. For every 3 quarts water add ½ tsp. salt and 1 Tbs. oil. No matter what kind of pasta —do not over cook. The timing can only be gauged by tasting — not once but several times. The state of "al dente" is reached when no taste of raw flour remains and yet the pasta still offers slight resistance to the bite. When pasta is "al dente" remove immediately with pasta scoop or drain in colander. If serving plain, pour into bowl and gently loss with olive oil. May season with salt, garlic and/or parsley to taste.

THE PROTEIN MYTH

When too much of a good thing is a bad thing.
by Mervyn G. Hardinge, M.D., and William C. Andress, D.H.Sc.

It all started in the middle of the nineteenth century. The seeds were sown by Dr. Justus von Liebig, one of the most famous German chemists of the time. His renown stemmed from having developed a method of determining the amount of protein in plant and animal tissue. Though somewhat refined, his method is still used today. But Liebig made a big mistake. Observing that muscles are made up largely of protein, he assumed that protein must be their primary fuel. Thus he proclaimed, "Muscle strength depends on the amount of protein eaten."

Sometime later, one of his proteges, Dr. Karl Voit, noted that the daily diet of laborers and soldiers contained on average 118 grams, or four ounces, of protein. He reasoned that since these men were big, strong, and muscular, they must be eating the ideal amount of protein. One hundred eighteen grams of protein per day became Voit's standard requirement for protein, a standard that quickly gained international acceptance.

But across the Atlantic, at Yale University, Dr. Russell Chittenden wasn't convinced. He wondered, "Should the amount of protein be more? or should it be less?"

In other words, was 118 grams what the body required -- or simply what these hardworking men happened to be eating? To find out, he studied soldiers and athletes under a variety of situations.

After years of careful research he found that 40 to 60 grams of protein, or less than half the amount recommended by Voit, was more than adequate, even for hardworking men. But by this time Voit's standard was so well established that little attention was paid to Chittenden's findings.

In fact, many people still believe that a high-protein diet is the healthiest way to eat. Now, don't get me wrong. Protein is a vital component of everyone's diet. That cannot be disputed. The myth isn't about the need for protein, but rather over the touting of protein as the

most essential dietary item, especially in terms of strength and endurance.

In order to dispel this error, it is helpful to know the proper role of protein in the body. Next to water, protein is the main substance in plant and animal cells (with the exception of fat cells).

In young animals, growth is a result of the increase in the number of cells. The faster an animal grows, the more rapidly cells must be manufactured, and thus more protein must be available to support this rapid growth.

Take a look at Table 1. It shows the growth rate of a human from birth to maturity. Notice that growth is not always constant. During the first year of life, growth is faster than it is during the second, which is faster than during the third, and so on. Growth rate levels off during the early school years, then during adolescence there is another growth spurt.

The body's need for protein varies in conjunction with these changes in growth rate. When growth is rapid and vast numbers of new cells are being formed, the demand for protein is high. But when maturity is reached, protein needs lessen. This is because adults don't need protein for growth. They need protein only for maintenance and, in the

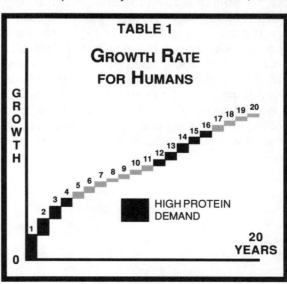

TABLE 1

GROWTH RATE FOR HUMANS

GROWTH

HIGH PROTEIN DEMAND

20 YEARS

case of injury, for repair of damaged tissues. Thus, to a large extent, the amount of protein needed depends on how rapidly growth is taking place.

Table 2 shows a list of common domestic animals, arranged according to the time it takes for the newborn of each species to double its birth weight.

Humans grow slower than any other animal. A newborn baby takes 180 days to double its birth weight. In comparison, a horse grows three times as fast, doubling its birth weight in just 60 days. And the cat is faster still, doubling its birth weight in just seven days. This is 26 times faster than the growth of the human baby.

Nature has accounted for these varying growth rates in a most interesting way. On a percentage basis, human milk contains the lowest amount of protein, averaging just 1.4 percent during the early weeks of infancy. On the other hand, the milk the mare feeds her colt contains 2 percent protein. The mother cat provides her kittens a much higher level of protein -- 9.5 percent. So if anyone would like a protein jog, just drink a glass of cat's milk.

But remember, the 1.4 percent protein in the woman's breast milk is an average. Research has shown that the protein content of human milk lessens week by week to accommodate the slowing growth rate of the infant. Beginning with a high of 2 percent during the first week after birth, the protein drops to 1.2 percent at the end of 8 weeks and then later levels off at around 1 percent.

Yet, what do we do? As soon as baby Wally is weaned we place him on the higher-protein cow's milk and feed it to him for the rest of his life. Since an eight-ounce glass of milk contains eight grams of protein, it's easy to see how in the course of a day milk can be a major source of protein.

Over the past 70 years, more and more research has shown the fallacy of the high-protein standard that Voit advocated. Currently the Nutrition Board of the National Research Council of the United States recommends 56 grams of protein per day for the average man, and 44 grams for women. For many years the World Health Organization of the United Nations has advocated 50 grams of protein per day, recognizing that even this amount provides a generous margin of safety. An unrefined diet easily provides this amount or more, even when no animal products are eaten.

I once had a cocky graduate student who failed to take a particular class seriously. He made it a habit to come late to class, and even began to skip classes. One day I called him into my office. I reminded him of my policy that if a student missed class sessions he would have to make them up by completing a project that dealt with the material covered in the missed sessions.

I then proceeded to give him an assignment of designing a low-protein diet (30 grams or less) that would meet the nutrient requirements for the average 30-year-old male who ate 2,500 calories.

"A piece of cake," laughed the rebellious student as he left my office.

One week later he returned griping about the unfairness and the impossibility of the assignment I had given him. You see, protein is one of the easiest nutrients to get in the diet. When enough calories are available from unrefined foods, it is almost impossible to create a protein deficiency.

In fact, the typical American diet, which is too high in protein (the average is more than 100 grams a day, and many get much more than this), may actually do more harm than good.

Dr. Chittenden said it well: "Any excess over and beyond what is really needed is not only uneconomical, but may be directly injurious. This is especially true of the protein foods."

More recently, Dr. Barry Brenner from Harvard University says, "There is a fundamental mismatch between the design of the human kidney and the burden imposed on it by the high-protein diet of the average American or Westerner."

He is referring to the fact that exess dietary protein places added burdens on the kidneys, thereby contributing to premature loss of kidney function even in otherwise healthy people.

Studies have shown that high-protein diets cause animals to grow faster and mature earlier. Unfortunately, those animals also die sooner.

A final argument against a high-protein diet lies in the very design of the human body. Humans were not designed anatomically nor physiologically to eat high-protein diets. Our digestive system most nearly resembles that of animals that are primarily fruit eaters. The original diet provided by the Creator for the occupants of the Garden of Eden is the best today and therefore still recommended. It is a high-complex-carbohydrate, low-protein, low-fat regimen.

Liebig and Voit were great scientists, but as Dr. Hindhede from the Hindhede Laboratory of Nutrition Research said, "The errors of great men are a hundred times more dangerous than the nonsense of the multitude."

The errors of these men have not died easily. But over the years the cracks have been exposed. With the weight of current scientific evidence the protein myth is being crumbled.

Dr. Mervyn G. Hardinge, founder and dean emeritus of the School of Public Health at Loma Linda University, is now director of Health Productions, a department in the university that produces slide/tape and video transfer programs on health topics William Andress, D.H.Sc., M.P.H., is production manager for Health Productions.

Adapted from *Vibrant Life* Jan./Feb. 1990.

TABLE 2

PROTEIN CONTENT OF MILK OF DIFFERENT SPECIES AS RELATED TO RATE OF GROWTH*

Species	Time (Days) to Double Birth Weight	Protein (Percent)
Man	180	1.4
Horse	60	2.0
Cow	47	3.4
Goat	19	3.3
Pig	18	5.9
Sheep	10	5.5
Dog	8	7.1
Cat	7	9.5

*Data Chiefly from Bunge, G.: Textbook of Physiological and Pathological Chemistry, 2nd ed. (English) Philadelphia: P. Blakiston's Son and Co., 1902.

DIETARY FAT — GOOD OR BAD?

by Bernell E. Baldwin, Ph.D.

Did you realize that you eat more than one-fourth pound of pure fat everyday, — more than a hundred pounds[1] each year, — if you are an average American? More than one thousand calories worth, — at least thirty to forty percent of your diet, — this is a lot of fat, a rich diet indeed!

Each person in the developing nations, on the other hand, eats only thirty pounds of fat a year, or approximately fourteen percent of his total daily food as measured in calories.

Could this difference in the amount of fat consumed have anything to do with the fact that there are many more heart attacks and cancers in the affluent nations than in the developing areas of the world? Is fat bad? How much, if any, should we eat? What kind should it be?

Importance of Fats

We need some fat. The right fats are necessary and even essential for the structure and function of every cell of the human body.[2] They are made from small molecules called fatty acids, which we eat in our foods or our bodies make from other materials. Some fatty acids that we cannot make are so valuable that they are called essential. Fats are fuels, — in fact they are the most concentrated source of energy we can get; they give us twice as much as any other food. They also serve as banks to store energy in our bodies. Insulation is another very important function. Fats insulate us thermally protecting us from cold, and electrically, in that every nerve of our bodies is insulated with at least some fat. They are also necessary for mechanical protection of the body. The right kinds of fats can help remove cholesterol from arteries. The fat-soluble vitamins, from the A, D, E and K groups come in, are used and stored in our bodies with fat. Aesthetically, dietary fat contributes to the taste and satisfaction of food and is essential for the attractive appearance of the human body. The relation of dietary fats to health, then, is a matter of how much fat we eat, and what kind. We need to get all the advantages good fats bring and eliminate the dual problems of too much and unhealthful fat.

What are Fats?
Where are They Found?

Fats are oily greasy materials, and those we eat are found in abundance in meats, animal and dairy products including cheese, eggs, nuts and other seeds, oils and salad dressings. Invisible fat is usually added in baking, generally cooking and, of course frying, and so is hidden by food preparation. Most dietary fat is invisible.

If this isn't tricky enough, the body can make large amounts of fat, and saturated at that, from excess carbohydrate and protein in the diet. Also, almost all foods usually eaten, even lettuce, have some fat.

How are Oils Processed?

Years ago, oil seeds or animal fat sources were prepared by mechanical processing with or without heat.[3] Currently in America, the fat is dissolved in a chemical, as hexane. Then the mixture is heated, thus separating the oil from the hexane, which can be recycled. Typically the next step in the refining process uses caustic soda or soda ash and phosphoric acid. Next, the fat is bleached with acid-treated diatomaceous earth, — and sometimes with charcoal. Deodorizing is usually accomplished by using live steam at temperatures of 400-470 degrees for one to two hours. Winterizing is the process of removing from the oil substances that would solidify at cold temperatures.

Hydrogenation is the next step. This process uses heat, pressure and a bit of nickel to force hydrogen into the molecules of the oil, thus destroying the valuable unsaturated double bonds of the fat and saturating them and distorting the shape of the molecules.

Additives are often used for a variety of purposes. To help emulsify fats for baked goods, mono-and diglycerides are often added. Polysorbate 80 is sometimes added to help oils blend with vinegar or acetic acid. In a further attempt to delay rancidity (oxidation), anti-oxidants such as BHA and BHT are often added. Methyl silicone is sometimes added to decrease foaming and oxidation in oils used for deep fat frying. Phosphoric and citric acids may also be added to attach and remove copper and iron by a process called chelation.

How Does Processing Affect the Nutritional Value of Fats?

Conventional processing reduces the nutritive value of oils in the following ways:

1. The amount of polyunsaturated fatty acids, especially linolenic acid, is reduced drastically by the refining process. This essential fatty acid should help reduce blood clots and spasms in blood vessels in a way that has been recognized only recently. There is among the regulatory chemicals of our bodies a family of hormone-like substances called "prostaglandins" (PGs). Some of these are excitatory (PGEs); and are involved in the formation of blood clots, spasm of arteries, asthma, arthritis and many other abnormal body processes. Other PGs are inhibitory (PGIs) because, among other effects, they cause arteries to relax and help prevent these problems. Linolenic acid fosters the formation of greater amounts of PGIs and less of PGEs. It is very sensitive and easily destroyed by hydrogenation.

2. The actual shape of the molecules is changed. The unsaturated part of a molecule of fat forms a hinge that helps make the fat more fluid. Because molecules of fatty acids make up most of cell membranes, keeping them fluid is very significant in permitting minerals and trace elements needed by the cells to pass through the cell membranes. Hydrogenation tends to hamper this transportation system. Cells get too stiff and it is easier for cancer viruses to invade.

3. Most of the molecules of any unsaturated fatty acid are so shaped that the arms of the molecule project in the same direction. This is called the "cis" (pronounced "sis") form. At the double bond hydrogenation turns one of the arms of many of the molecules in the opposite direction, creating a much greater amount of the "trans" form. Unfortunately, consumption of large amounts of the trans form may cause its accumulation in the heart. But the heart cannot use this form to make energy as well as it can use better quality fat.

4. Refining removes significant amounts of the vitamins that come with the fat in its natural state. Normally we get these vitamins in our food sources and the fat cells of our bodies store them for future need. Vitamin A, that helps prevent some cancers, is cut down severely by processing. Vitamins of the E group[2] are powerful antioxidants, that is, they prevent chemi-

cal changes that take place in stored fats when they become rancid as well as chemical changes associated with cancer in the body.

5. Anti-oxidants other than those of the vitamin E group are reduced.

6. Oil seeds contain significant amounts of minerals and trace elements. Processing eliminates these almost entirely.

7. Plant sterols are removed. These are good relatives of cholesterol, and resemble it so much that they fit into the gates through which cholesterol would otherwise enter, blocking its entrance into the blood. Plant sterols themselves are not absorbed to any significant extent. The end result is that cholesterol levels throughout the blood are reduced.

8. Lecithins are removed. This is unfortunate, because lecithins provide a component for the use in the body of an enzyme called LCAT (lecithin-cholesterol acyl transferase). LCAT is one of the biochemical heroes that actually helps remove cholesterol deposits from within the blood vessels.

The high temperatures that are used in modern oil processing also tend to form new hybrid molecules. Some of these by-products have not been studied carefully enough for us to assure the consumer that they are safe. It is true that the fat industry has sponsored research showing that pigs will live apparently normal lives on high levels of the new fats. But negative results from some experiments have confused the issue.

On the positive side, does oil processing confer any benefits? Yes.[3] While it decreases the nutritive value of good oil sources, it also removes mold carcinogens (cancer-forming chemicals) and poisons from dangerous sources such as moldy corn or peanuts. Other harmful constituents and toxins[3] are not only practically eliminated from the oil but the oils are prevented from becoming rancid by destruction of substances like linolenic acid. In short, if the original raw source of fat is old, dirty, cheap, or undesirable, refining is helpful.

The Bottom Line

Oil and fat technology need an entirely new perspective based on health. We have done to fats what in the past we did to sugars and to flours, — we have compromised their virtues and multiplied their vices. Surely, in view of our present urgent need for disease prevention, our supplies of fat need very thorough scrutiny and, where necessary, marked improvement.

Fats, Heart and Blood Vessel Disease

Scientists agree that excess fat eaten in the diet can contribute to excess heart and blood vessel disease. How can fat cause heart attacks? Our American yearly average intake of one hundred pounds of fat often ends up as too much fat in the blood. Saturated fat is a well-known contributor to atherosclerosis.[4] Cholesterol eaten in foods from animal sources makes its own smaller contribution to the cholesterol load in the body. Many people do not realize that each of us makes from an eighth to a quarter of a teaspoonful of pure cholesterol daily. This is more than we need. Any extra we eat, as such, increases significantly the total cholesterol in the body. Our luxurious eating of fat-rich diets has a lot to do with the leading cause of death in America today, — heart and blood vessel disease.[4]

New Cholesterol Villains

The account of how Dr. C.B. Taylor and his fellow workers of the VA Medical Center in Albany, New York, discovered some new cholesterol villains is most interesting. As a grant that supported his research was running out he rushed out and got a hundred pounds of cholesterol, planning to use it for years in less funded research. But from one year to the next it seemed that his results would not agree. So he had his supply of old cholesterol, which had undergone chemical oxidation, chemically analyzed and discovered three very potent breakdown products of cholesterol.[4] Minute amounts of oxidized forms of cholesterol can kill the smooth muscle cells of arteries in five hours time. With a scanning electron microscope he found that after he injected small amounts of these oxidized forms into rabbits, the arteries were severely damaged. This new information adds a new essential link to our understanding of heart disease, because the destruction of smooth muscle cells in the walls of arteries is a key step in the production of cholesterol deposits, or plaques, leading to heart attacks. It tells us that, whereas excess ordinary cholesterol is dangerous enough for the arteries of the body, these new forms of oxidized cholesterol are much more deadly.

Where are the New Cholesterol Villains Found?

Using a special research technique called chromatography, Dr. Taylor found these same kinds of oxidized cholesterol in some common foods:[5] lard, ripened cheese, pancake mix, powdered eggs and custards. He even found one of these oxidized cholesterols in one infant formula. A person acquainted with Biblical instruction immediately thinks of Leviticus 11:7, which, more than 3000 years before the discovery of cholesterol, forbade eating swine's flesh. And the pioneer nutrition writer, E.G. White, counselled in 1869, "Cheese is still more objectionable, it is wholly unfit for food.[6]

So we now know that besides unsaturated fats going rancid with aging, cholesterol also is sensitive to oxidation. This gives us two strong reasons for being careful about the sources, purity and freshness of all fat products

Some Fats are Friendly to the Heart and Blood

In our blood there are special little particles called HDL (high-density lipoprotein) that scavenge the cholesterol out from the nooks and crannies of the body and take it back to the liver for disposal. Oleic acid, found in olives, seems to help maintain or perhaps increase HDL concentration. Exercise is another important way to maintain or increase your HDL level.

Diets containing increased amounts of special unsaturated fatty acids called "omega 3 acids"[5] can help balance the fats in the body and in the blood. Platelets (blood particles that carry clotting chemicals) are reduced in the number and less inflamed. We have already mentioned the balancing of PGs by linolenic acid; one of the most significant of these omega-3 acids. See the accompanying chart of fats for useful sources of omega-3 fat. Especially valuable plant sources are flax, soy, turnips, spinach, beans, bananas, rye and nuts. Under some circumstances, omega-3 fats can help somewhat in reducing breast and colon cancer.[7]

Dr. Connor, of Oregon, is using salmon oil and salmon flesh as a dietary source of omega-3 but fish has some problems. Fish all too often may carry cancer-causing viruses. It contains cholesterol, and possibly oxidized cholesterol and malondialdehyde[8] (MDA), a harmful breakdown product of fat.[6] Fish oil tends not only to form the dangerous MDA but also to increase formation of foam cells in the development of atherosclerosis.[9]

Of course, there is a cluster of other risk factors we have to deal with in any overall program for prevention of heart attacks: cigarette smoking, high-blood pressure, cholesterol control, regular balanced exercise, steady stress control and appropriate check-ups by a prevention-oriented physician.

Fat and Learning

Dr. Galli, of the University of Milan, Italy, found that tallow, a saturated animal fat, reduced the rate and level of learning in mice. For comparison, olive fat did not decrease the efficiency of their learning.

Fats and Cancer

Now for the sixty-four dollar question: what is the relationship of dietary fat to cancer?

Dr. K.K. Carroll, from the University of Western Ontario, Canada, points out that diets rich in fats are under heavy suspicion as contributing causes of cancer.[10] Well-known studies of migrant Japanese revealed that as they move from Japan (where the occurrence of cancer is very low) to Hawaii and then to Los Angeles, the amount of cancer increases move by move until their cancer rate approaches that of the United States. Unfortunately, even the Japanese in Japan are gradually getting more cancer of the breast and colon as they eat richer diets.

There are from 8-200 times more cancer in some countries than in others, therefore environment must be the major factor in developing these kinds of cancer. And fat is the most important environmental factor.

Cancer of the breast seems to be peculiarly sensitive to unsaturated fatty acids as found in corn or vegetable oils.[7] On a high-fat diet laboratory animals had no more cancer when they ate unsaturated fat than when they ate saturated fat. But on a low-fat diet, the unsaturated fatty acids promoted more cancers. The evidence was clear that the more fat consumed, the more cancer produced. Also, the less fat consumed, the fewer tumors produced. Since cancer growth rates were reduced by low fat diets, proper nutrition should be a definite part of any plan for treatment of cancer.

When research animals are fed both high-fat and high-protein at the same time they develop more cancers than when fed only high-fat or high-protein. When 40% of the calories (20% of the diet by weight) came from beef tallow, more cancer developed than when the same concentration of corn oil was given.[8]

Young animals and little people need more protein to grow with than the old ones need just to keep going. Higher protein levels for developing animals were not detrimental, — as a matter of fact, they increased the resistance to cancer. But later on in life a high protein diet decreased the resistance to cancer.

Studies in research labs give us four lines of evidence that relate excess fat consumption to increased cancer risk: (1) virus-caused cancer is promoted by excess fat. (2) chemical-caused cancer is promoted by excess fat, (3) cancer secondary to x-ray radiation is promoted by excess fat, and (4) when transplantable tumors are put into animals and carefully followed, excess fat worsens the cancer problem. The fact that a high-fat, high-protein diet produced the worst possible cancer risk agrees with the fact that American and Western European populations that are on the richest diets get the most cancer. When four different cancer causing chemicals were tested, all produced even more cancer when given to animals on a high-fat diet.

Some bile acids can produce bowel cancer. Furthermore, the richer the diet is, the more bile acids and breakdown products of bile salts there are. Careful comparisons were made of these bile salts and irritating chemicals in various groups. In New York meat-eating subjects, and in Seventh-day Adventist vegetarians from New York, it was shown that the vegetarians produced less bile acids in the bowel. The Seventh-day Adventist vegetarians ate 28% less fat and 2.5 times more fiber.[11] This probably helps explain their lower cancer rates.

Calories do Count

In all fairness, we need to realize that fat and protein aren't the whole story. Excess of calories is a very important factor for the production of cancer.

Fat and Immunity

One way that diet influences cancer has to do with the immune system. This is the "national guard" of the body, ready and standing by to resist any invaders. In the blood there are several different kinds of fat particles that can reduce or interfere with the function of our immune systems. These particles are the very low density lipoproteins (VLDL), and the intermediate lipoprotein fractions (IDL).[9] Blood levels of both are increased by a fat-rich diet, hence it appears that such a diet can lead to reduced resistance to disease. This may have a bearing on resistance to germs in general and cancer in particular.

Good News About Olives

Until recently, we have seemed to be on the horns of a real dilemma. Excess saturated fats on one hand tend to produce increased blood vessel disease, whereas excess unsaturated fats, such as from corn oil, on the other hand, can produce cancer risk. But now, — olives to the rescue! They seem to produce neither as much trouble with the heart and blood vessels or from decreased resistance to cancer.[10] Olive-eating peoples clustering around the Mediterranean Sea are famous for their much lower incidence of heart attacks, although they may take in the same amount of fats as other populations eating other fats.

Many diets suggested for preventing coronary heart disease lower high density lipo-proteins in the blood. But HDLs protect us from atherosclerosis. Oleic acid, as from olives, tends to maintain HDL levels, and thus would improve one's ability to deal with cholesterol in the body. Adding moderate amounts of olives to our diet, then, is a good way to provide valuable fat without increasing the risk of heart attack on the one hand or, possibly, increased cancer risk on the other. Avocados, almonds, walnuts and others are good sources.

How Much Vegetable Fat?

The amount of vegetable fat we need depends on a number of factors:

Age. The tiny, busy bodies of babies thrive on the higher levels of fats found normally in mother's milk. Ordinarily, adults do not need that much fat.

Occupation. Young hard-working men thrive on a richer diet than sedentary people can handle.

Exercise. People who engage in much steady physical exercise can burn up more fat.

Climate. The colder the climate that we live in (not just look out at through double-glazed windows), the more fat we need and profitably burn up in our activities in the colder air.

Hormone status. Thyroid, adrenal, pancreatic and other hormone sources all can influence the utilization of fat by our bodies.

Other special conditions. People are different. Thus, it is neither wise nor efficient to try to come up with some magic figure of a certain percent of fat that every one must eat. What we need are principles, not pigeon holes, and wisdom, not slogans.

Special Dangers for Older People

As people get older their rate of metabolism steadily slows. Thus, diets suitable for very active youngsters or younger adults can contribute sooner or later, to very serious problems such as obesity, atherosclerosis, diabetes and cancer in oldsters.

Perspectives

Thus, discriminating moderation is the key to the fat question. Living conventional, fashionable lives, eating rich fashionable meals, and then dying fashionable deaths is not the way to go! Solomon, the wise man, wrote, "The curse causeless shall not come."[11] And cancer for sure is a curse. We need to serve foods that are a delight to the eyes, pleasant to the taste and truly health-promoting.

The practical way to deliver the new nutrition to the people is to give them something better.

Vegetable Fats are "Something Better"

Vegetable fats are "something better" physically. They are more liquid. This helps the membranes of all your more than 100 trillion cells be more flexible and dynamic. This is especially crucial in the brain, to say nothing of your heart and blood vessels.

Vegetable fats also are "something better" chemically. Analysis of the major fatty acid components of pork, beef, and chicken shows them to be the reverse of those of fruits, vegetables, nuts and seeds. Since we are what we eat, we need to think this through. Eating first-hand food will tend to make us first-hand chemically, instead of second-hand, — filled with saturated fat and deficient in the monos and the polys.

Vegetable fats are "something better" physiologically. They improve the ability of the cells of the body to exchange materials between the cells and their environment, thus enabling them to move cholesterol out more effectively.[(13)] Vegetable fats are "something better" nutritionally because they keep better company. No cholesterol. No virus.

Vegetable fats are "something better" for the brain. They not only help build the more flexible membranes but vegetable fats come with vegetable proteins. They are cleaner. The blood tends to get too many breakdown products from animal foods. These can interfere with the brain electrically.[(14)]

So vegetable fats are "something better," period. Populations using more vegetable fats and few or no animal fats have less heart and blood vessel disease, and less cancer.

In the sixth century B.C., "Daniel purposed in his heart that he would not defile himself with the portion of the king's meat" (Daniel 1:8). Instead he requested "vegetables to eat" (Daniel 1:12, RSV). His diet, as modern as today, contributed to his rapid advancement to become prime minister and statesman of the world empire of Babylon.

Conclusions and Recommendations

Boldly outlined are these facts. The right fats in the right amounts are absolutely essential for every cell of the body. Conventional refining processes inevitably and significantly damage the nutritive content, and hence value, of fats. Hydrogenation is unhealthful. Fat-rich diets contribute unquestionably to cancer, coronary heart disease and heart attacks, obesity and diabetes. Animal fats are especially damaging to arteries and are incriminated in bowel, breast and other cancers in human beings. Excess of even vegetable fats is dangerous. Olives contain more oleic acid and have lower risks of heart disease and possibly of cancer. Fats as they occur naturally in plants are superior; go very easy on oils. The ideal diet would provide an abundance of whole grain products, fruits, vegetables and moderate amounts of nuts and oil seeds. "White" oils belong with white sugar and white flour. A variety of natural, unrefined vegetable fats, free of excess heating and unhydrogenated, served in discriminating moderation, is best. Surely it would be wise to read labels, — many people pay dearly for not reading the "fine print." Some labels could truthfully say "This produce may be hazardous to your health!" Vigorous daily exercise will help our bodies use, rather than suffer from, the fat we eat.

We will all need to develop new insights, progressive understanding, new attitudes, new recipes and steady eating patterns. Thus we can help renew our cells, tissues and organs to their maximum efficiency. Happy, abundant living is not an accident, it is an achievement..

Some Vegetarian Sources of Linolenic Acid

Food	Unit	mg
Linseed (flax) oil	1 Tbsp.	1,961
Walnuts, English	10 halves	1,024
Soybean oil	1 Tbsp.	1,006
Spinach, canned	1 cup	559
Soybeans, cooked	1/2 cup	360
Turnips, mashed	1 cup	289
Apple	1 medium	108
Avocado pear	1/2 California	74
Sweet potatoes, mashed	1 cup	69
Safflower seed	1 Tbsp.	68
Chestnuts	10 nuts	46
Banana	1 banana	43
Wheat germ	1 Tbsp.	42
Peanuts	10 lg. or 12 sm. 1 Tbsp.	36
Potatoes, cooked	1 cup	34
Rye, flour	1/4 cup	33
Almonds	10 almonds	27
Cucumber, pared, diced	1 cup	26
Bread, whole meal, wheat	1 slice	25
Barley, dry	1/6 cup	21

References

1. Staff, Dietary Fats and Health. Journal of the American Oil Chemists Society. 58:835a, 1981.
2. Tocantins, L.M., The Mammalian Blood Platelet in Health and Disease. Medicine 17:155, 1938.
3. Staff, Effects of Processing on the Nutritive Value of Fats and Oils Used in Human Nutrition. In Dietary Fats and Oils In Human Nutrition: A Joint FA/WHO Report. pp. 37-45, Food and Agriculture Organization of the United Nations. Rome 1978, pp. 37-45.
4. Levy, R.M., and M. Feinleib, Risk Factors for Coronary Artery Disease and their Management. Heart Disease, E. Braunwald, ed., Saunders, Phila., 1980, pp. 1246-1248.
5. Taylor, D.B., S-K Peng, et al. Spontaneously Occurring Angiotoxic Derivatives of Cholesterol, Am. J. Clin. Nutr. 32:40-57, 1979.
6. White, E.G. Cheese. Counsels on Diet and Foods Review and Herald Publ Assoc., Washington, D.C., 1938, pp. 368-369.
7. Rupa, P.O. and R.A. Karmali. Dietary Effects of Omega-3 Fatty Acids on The Growth of the R3230AC Mammary Tumor. Fed. Proc. 45:1089, 1986. O'Connor, T.P. and F. Peterson, et al. Influence of Dietary Menhaden Oil on 7, 12-Dimethylbenzanthracene Induced Mammary Tumorigenesis in Rats. Fed. Proc. 45:1089, 1986.
8. Marnett, L.J. and M.A. Tuttle. Comparison of the Mutagenicities of Malondialdenhyde and the Side Products Formed During its Chemical Synthesis. Cancer Research, 40:276-282, 1980.
9. Rogers, K.A. and M.J. Karnovsky. Dietary Fish Oil Enhancers Hypercholesterolemia-Induced Monocyte Adhesion and Foam Cell Formation in the Rat Thoracic Aorta. Fed. Proc. 45:813, 1986.
10. Carroll, K.K. Dietary Factors in Hormone-Dependent Cancers. Nutrition and Cancer. M. Winick, ed. Wiley & Sons, N.Y., 1977, pp. 25-40.
11. Reddy, B.S. Bile Salts and Other Constituents of the Colon as Tumor Promoters, in Banbury Report 7. Gastrointestinal Cancer: Endogenous Factors. R.W. Bruce, ed., Cold Spring Harbor Laboratory; pp. 345-363, 1981.
12. White, E.G. Olives. Counsels on Diet and Foods, Review and Herald Pub. Assoc., Washington, D.C., 1938, pp. 359-369.
13. Bloj, B. and D.B. Zilversmit. Complete Exchangeability of Cholesterol in Phosphatidylcholine/Cholesterol Vesicles of Different Degrees of Unsaturation. Biochemistry, 16:3943-3947, 1977.

INDEX

INDEX

INDEX

187

INDEX

NOTES

NOTES

NOTES